Anchored

Jodi Luberto

TRILOGY CHRISTIAN PUBLISHERS
Tustin, CA

Trilogy Christian Publishers
A Wholly Owned Subsidiary of Trinity Broadcasting Network
2442 Michelle Drive
Tustin, CA 92780

Anchored

Copyright © 2024 by Jodi Luberto

Scripture quotations marked (NKJV) are taken from the New King James Version®. Copyright © 1982 by Thomas Nelson. Used by permission. All rights reserved.

For information, address Trilogy Christian Publishing Rights Department, 2442 Michelle Drive, Tustin, CA 92780.

Trilogy Christian Publishing/TBN and colophon are trademarks of Trinity Broadcasting Network.

For information about special discounts for bulk purchases, please contact Trilogy Christian Publishing.

Trilogy Disclaimer: The views and content expressed in this book are those of the author and may not necessarily reflect the views and doctrine of Trilogy Christian Publishing or the Trinity Broadcasting Network.

10 9 8 7 6 5 4 3 2 1

Library of Congress Cataloging-in-Publication Data is available.

ISBN: 979-8-89333-406-7

ISBN: 979-8-89333-407-4 (ebook)

This book is dedicated in loving memory of my mother, Annette Cozzolino, who always believed in me and always prayed for me.

Acknowledgments

I would like to give special thanks to Lisa
for all the heartfelt prayers.
Gina for helping me make this all happen,
and your encouragement.
Lynn and Kenny, here's to all the years of friendship.
David, thank- you for all that you did for me.

Most of all The Holy Spirit for leading, guiding and
directing me in every step.

Contents

Introduction vii
Chapter 1. 1
Chapter 2. 9
Chapter 3. 26
Chapter 4. 42
Chapter 5. 55
Chapter 6. 60
Chapter 7. 87
Chapter 8. 100
Chapter 9. 113
Chapter 10. 138
Chapter 11. 147
Chapter 12. 155
About the Author. 175

Introduction

My name is Jodi Ann Luberto, and I was born on February 3rd, 1968. I am from Belleville, New Jersey. I am a High School graduate class of 1986.While in high school, I studied cosmetology during my junior and senior year. Soon after I graduated, I went on to take my state board test for cosmetology and was then licensed in 1986.

My mother and father were divorced when I was just a child, and as far as I can remember I always have had a yearning to know God. Being a little girl and going to the Catholic Church, I somehow knew I wanted to learn more about God, so I left the Catholic Church and was introduced to Bethel Assembly of God church. After a few times of attending church services three times a week including Sunday evening and attending weekly Bible studies I felt this was the best choice for me, to stay within the Christian church. It was on a Sunday night where I got saved. I went up to the alter and I can still remember the elders and the pastoral staff laying hands on me and praying with me. It was then that I asked Jesus into my life. All I felt was the tears rolling down my cheeks and for the first time I felt so much love around me. I was overjoyed. Soon enough I was water baptized and I vowed to Jesus that I will always praise Him and dwell in the house of the Lord.

When I was sixteen years old, I was referred to go to another Christian church where I could make Christian friends, so I got involved with the youth group which also gave me the opportunity to be in the music ministry. Being in the music ministry has taught me true worship, which to me was more than just a song being sung. I knew back then this would be my calling. Being a Christian in school was tough for me because I had to carefully choose my friends and I was not able to participate in the things that kids do such as house parties and drinking or drugs I never had a desire to do any of those things. I can remember kids in my class would make fun of me because I would go to church on Friday nights while they were all talking about all of the partying they were planning to do.

Chapter 1

I started working at the age of thirteen at a McDonald's after school so that I could help my mom out with money because she needed it for things like food and clothing for me and my brother. After my mom and dad divorced, my dad never really saw his children and never paid his child support which made it very difficult for my mom to raise two children on welfare and food stamps.

A few years later, I was working at a hair salon as a shampoo girl while waiting for my cosmetology license. While working one day, I was leaning over the sink and I felt a sharp pain in my back and had a very hard time standing straight up so that day after I left work, I went to the hospital where I was admitted for seven days and put into traction for a slipped disc in my lower back. Unfortunately, the doctors came into my room and informed me that I now have a herniated disc and that whatever I was doing for work I must not do anymore, or I was going to be in pain the rest of my life. Following thereafter I had to start chiropractic care three to four times a week.

Being a young woman and having to go through something like this to have a bad back and still must find work that I can do without the strenuous lifting or bending. This was when I really started praying to God for healing because I knew this was going to be the cross that I had to bear so I was at every church service and always at Calvary asking for God to touch me and heal my lower back.

As I got older still and continued working for years, my back was always going to be a thorn in my side. I always felt the pain and it progressively became worse with arthritis, scoliosis, and bulging discs which inflicted a herniated disc which degenerated through the years.

My life was filled with physical pain, along with emotional issues and I have undergone many treatments including going to physical therapy and having to see pain management. With this, my faith grew because it drew me closer to Jesus and knowing Him, I trust that He knew my pain and my sufferings because according to His word in Isaiah (53:5, NKJV) which stated, "He was crushed for our iniquities the punishment that brought us peace was on him, and by his wounds we are healed." Which means that when Jesus died on the cross, everything we go through was literally nailed to the cross.

As for my personal life, I've dated and have had more than my share of boyfriends in my lifetime, call me a late bloomer, I started dating when I was twenty-two-years-old. I was engaged once which ended about a year later, but I can say now that relationship was no way part of God's will for my life. He was much older than myself and I was naïve and in love with the idea of being engaged. See, I always dreamed of having that perfect guy who would come to church with me. Along with having the white picket fenced house and do all the right things in front of the church congregation but in real life that wasn't the actual truth of what went on. Soon after he cheated, and we broke off the engagement just three weeks before the wedding date. Was I devastated? Or just in shock? Not totally sure, I just knew deep down in my heart something was not right so I did what anyone else in my place would do I said goodbye and broke all ties. I was crushed for some time at the thought of picking up my wedding gown on my last fitting day for me to tell the saleswomen, "Please put the dress in a box because there isn't going to be a wedding after all." I did have peace with God because I always prayed that He would protect my heart from being broken and if I did get my heart broken, He would put it back together. In time, He did just that it was well with my soul.

Several years later, I met someone when I was working for a health club called Bally Total Fitness. I became friends with this gentleman for about five years before we went out on a first date. At the time I recall he was dating someone, and I remember telling him I cannot and won't date you unless you end your relationship with this other female. Soon enough he came back with the words every young lady loves to hear, "I ended it with that women lets go out?" "Of course, now we can go out on a date." We fell madly in love with each other and that relationship lasted three years. During those times we spent a lot of time in the gym working out because we both shared so many common interests and that was the biggest one. One night, I was sitting watching TV when he glanced over at me and asked, "How would you like to go on vacation any place you choose?" I could not believe my ears after all I have never been outside the state of New Jersey, so we both agreed to take a trip to Cancun, Mexico for one week. Here we are at the airport we missed our first flight by like fifteen minutes or so we had no choice to get two connecting flights from Newark to Houston, TX then from Texas to Mexico which got us to Cancun six hours later. I remember getting off that plane and feeling the heat wave blast me in the face and we walked into customs. The heat was so hot I just wanted to get checked into our hotel just to turn the air conditioner on. The name of the resort was Miramar Mission a seven-story high building with every state flag on the front of the hotel and a huge swimming pool along with several hot tubs and a few steps following the pool was the beach breathtaking the beauty of the color of the ocean turquoise marine blue and almost white sand so fine it slips right through your toes when walking on it. The very next day I decided to get my hair braided, so that I didn't have to deal with doing my hair all over and over each day. The food was very good and so was the entertainment. I will never forget the times I had memorable and moments like that you don't want to forget. The Rainforest Cafe was one of the nicest places to have dinner along with the Hard Rock Café.

After the vacation was over, and I was back at my boyfriend's house looking at the pictures that we took I decided to get the best picture blown up. My only thought was *I'd like to put one of them into a frame for my wall in the bedroom.* It started getting late, so he took me home. When I was getting out of the car something came over me still to this day, I cannot describe what exactly the feeling was, but I suddenly looked back and waved goodbye as to say "goodnight." He then drove off.

It was the next morning when I thought I was having a terrible nightmare. My mom woke up in a lot of pain in her chest and fell on the floor I was so scared didn't know what was happening so I did what the only thing I knew to do was to call 911. An ambulance came and said mom had a heart attack. I then got into my car and went to the hospital. After a few hours I drove home from the hospital and the police pull my car over and asked me if they can talk with me. I got back to my home and they informed me that they were well aware that my mom was rushed to the hospital but this wasn't about her, it was about my boyfriend. They said that they received a call from the East Hanover police department and I should get in contact with them right away. There was nothing else could they tell me. So, I called the police department. They asked if I would come to the station for some questions in regard to my boyfriend I asked, "Why?" When we arrived at his house, he had passed away suddenly. I was a total wreck at this moment in time, on the other hand my mom was being transported to a heart hospital for immediate heart surgery. We were all so devastated with the news that I literally fell on the floor and stared screaming out of control. I felt as if my whole world came crashing down all around me and I then questioned God, *why this is happening? I can't handle all of this at the same time.* I was so nervous and in shock that my body went numb for a long time. I lost the most important person in my life and would have married him and now is gone there were no words that can ever describe the loss I felt and the tears I shed. My mom had to have stents put in her heart, but she would be okay. When she got back home, she was to take it easy for a while. In the meantime, I started taking care of her and looking out for her. She stopped driving at this point, so I took her to all of her doctors and food shopping etc. I became her caretaker.

I started working in retail which required me to have a flexible schedule working day and night, also every weekend. I did enjoy working loved being a sales associate it was long hours but even then, standing on cement floors wasn't good for my back at all. Each night, I would get home only to put the ice packs on it. That became difficult to bear after a long time of doing that. I decided to do retail part time and work for the gyms also part time so that was what I did.

During the fall, I took a drive through the mountains of Sussex County just to get out of my regular routine and to experience different scenery for a change. While on this long drive the trees looked so beautiful all the colors that they were and seeing the cows and horses on the way really makes you think that there are very nice places to see but as your driving the roads up and down the mountains have all kinds of turns and bends but the thing that I have noticed was that you can only see was what was in front of you. This is so true for the journey that we are all on. We can only look as far as the eye can see, the rest is believing what is ahead even if you can't see with the human eye, you would need to see it using spiritual eyes. We all have one thing in common and that is a destiny.

Some people tend to think that there is no such thing as destiny or a fine place to be at the end of the journey called life. Let me explain what I mean by this. We all were born with an innocence with no idea of what life was going to hold in store for us then we grow up. We all created our path in life with all the choices and decisions which brought us to where we are today. Not all our plans worked out and not all our dreams came to pass. I cannot speak for the rest of the world; I can only speak for myself. See, I am a dreamer, always was always will be. I have dreams of being a wealthy person even though I am not, I also have goals I'd like to achieve someday like having my own apartment, and I want to travel again and see more of the Caribbean islands again. So, the big question is destiny, the journey, or the destination? Is it the place where you wind up or the life you make for yourself? You can set goals and dreams even aspirations for yourself, but I feel that anything is possible, but you must want it although there are many times where you don't always get what you want. We will never have all the answers to life's hardest questions. But the most important thing is that you keep moving forward with the ideas and don't give up. Stay steadfast in the way you keep going in a direction that God will lead you to the place where your heart and soul meet. Then you will know what your destiny is.

Chapter 2

In 2012, my mom needed to have triple bypass surgery, so she went into the hospital and had the surgery. Two days later, she caught a very bad infection and her temperature skyrocketed to 109 degrees, she went septic and passed on. I was working at the time at the gym that morning when we got the call to go to the hospital right away. When we arrived, it was worse than a horror show. The curtain was closed, the nurses all playing on their cell phones laughing and joking around like nothing happened, I pulled the curtain to see my mom's eyes wide open! I was furious, I asked what was going on there, no one knew anything. Such a bad experience for me. I cannot even begin to imagine what happened to her while she was in that bed. Life for me hasn't been good at all so I wondered, *God, are you still there where did you go? How does one person handle so much loss in a lifetime and still have peace?* I had a hard time with mourning and depression, so I didn't want to go to church for a while or at least until I was ready to move on. At the time, I was attending Nutley Abundant Life regularly with my mom but most of the time I would go by myself.

I started watching TBN network to somehow get back to feeling normal again and to stir up my faith. I started praying for Jesus to lead me on and to guide me to find another church to go that I can grow spiritually and get my relationship with God back to where it was. I had to realize that my mom and boyfriend were both with Jesus and to give ALL my brokenness to the Lord. I have accepted it now and I allowed the Holy Spirit to keep ministering to my heart every day from then on. I remember what Jesus promised, "that he goes to prepare a place for us and if it weren't so he would have not said so." That Bible verse became more real to me as the years went on. I can recall praying God what church would you want me to go to? For six months then one day I was watching TBN, and I saw a pastor on there in which I hadn't seen in a long time, so I looked up the church to see where it was, I wrote down the address put it in my drawer. A few months later I was at a product testing facility and met a woman there who started talking with me very briefly then handed me her phone number then said, "We can go to her church one day." I then asked and she told me that her pastor was the same one in whom I watched six months ago on television. I said, "Yes I'd love to visit there very much." It was like a God appointment confirmation for me I felt the push to take her up on her offer to go. After attending this church service, I felt as if this was the place I should be going to. I was welcomed with open arms and a loving atmosphere. I was introduced to the pastor along with the staff. To this day, I am still attending there and being blessed at every service. I started taking Bible classes. I prayed to get back into the music ministry, it's something that's been in my heart for a very long time. To this day, this woman is a very dear friend to me.

In life you go through this journey with lots of narrow roads that don't make any sense when you're on them but when you trust in God to lead you, He will in His time. I truly believe that there are times where we will make the wrong choices or go down a different path, but the main thing is to keep moving forward even if you cannot see what's ahead just remember God said, "He is with you never to leave you or forsake you." He is always in the boat, meaning in every situation and circumstance He is with you, and you won't drown in the storm you're in. Every day I had to keep reading His word and learning faith scriptures to get me through the next day. I stood firm on this Bible verse, Hebrew. (11:6, NKJV) "Without Faith it is impossible to please God, anyone who comes to him must believe that he exists and that he rewards those who earnestly seek him." I'm not saying it was easy, no it wasn't at all, however it all came together when the Lord spoke to me and said, "My daughter, trust in Me. I will be your provider and source the sooner you realize that the easier things become." I can recall so many times when I thought God was nowhere to be found but I realized that He was there waiting all the time for me to just come to Him.

I was working for a retail store on weekends and working another job for a small mom and pop gym during the week. In about six months, the gym closed the business and I needed to work more hours, so I took a step of faith and asked for more hours at the store, and they said yes with no problem. I was there for about nine months or so. I loved working there, I was very good at what I did, and some say competitive, until one day I was called to the back human resources department having no idea of why. I proceeded to shut down my register and headed to HR. I was asked to have a seat they let me go. I was so upset I could hardly think it was devastating to me because they informed me that I did something wrong that I had no idea was a company policy because when they were giving the orientation, I wasn't able to attend due to the fact I was still at work at my other job. I was never informed of this, so they felt it was easier to let me go.

So, I asked Jesus please find me another job. Two weeks later I found another job that paid more, and I was hired immediately. The seasonal time had passed by so quickly that after it was over most of those employees were asked to leave but they pulled me to the side and gave me a raise and asked if I'd like to stay on permanent. So of course, I stayed there. After about seven months I put in for my vacation for August for ten days which was approved with no problem. During that time six months in I started having very bad pains in my low back again, so I was getting to the point where I had to take mats to put under my feet while being at the self-checkout cash registers because the floors were concrete and hard on the knees and back. I never called out to have perfect attendance, but the pain was getting severe, so I scheduled an appointment with my primary care physician on my day off. I went to see my doctor explained that the pain was very severe, and I felt as if my back was burning on fire and my feet were going numb up and down my spine, I couldn't stand up straight anymore. So, he gave me some muscle relaxers to take and told me that he wants me to get on temporary disability and to see pain management as soon as possible.

I did just that, I went to human resources, gave my note and explained I needed to go out on temporary disability until my back got better. Of course, they told me I couldn't get compensated so I did what anyone else in my situation would do. I called corporate headquarters myself, put in a claim and started getting paid. That wasn't easy either, but God made a way for me when I thought there was no way. I went to see pain management for some time. I also had to do physical therapy and chiropractic care. Here it was six months later I wasn't feeling any better- what should I do?

In the meantime, I had this vacation already booked and it was too late to cancel it, so I prayed and decided to go anyway. My best friend and I went to a travel agency. I wanted to have my one dream come true which was to go on a cruise. Ever since I was a young girl it was always a huge dream of mine to take a cruise, so I did it. I packed my ice pack bag with me and my meds and off we went. It was a nine-day Royal Caribbean cruise. We sailed to Bermuda, St. Martin, San Juan, Puerto Rico, then to Labadie Haiti. We also booked three beach excursions to the islands. I said to myself as to my friend "let's just call this cruise therapy." She burst out laughing, she almost fell on the floor and giggled.

Let me explain what I mean by the therapy part and exactly what transpired in my own words. I figured out that it was going to be a long hard journey with physical therapy and all sorts of doctors and then having to eventually apply for permanent disability if I'm not feeling better after the six months of temporary disability, so I am going to use every part of everything this cruise has to offer to my knowledge to my advantage to try to help myself feel no pain aside from filling my ice bag up each night and taking muscle relaxers to calm the nerves in my back.

So here goes what a real vacation should always be, we pull up to this huge ship I can't believe how big this vessel is I say to my best friend, "Wow this is it I'm in total shock of the size I still cannot imagine that I actually am here." She replied, "Let's go give the luggage to the men and get checked in because it may take a while." It went very smoothly; the check-in process was great; hardly a wait. We received the room keys but couldn't go to the rooms until two hours later, so we walked around the cruise for a while checking it all out. I can still remember I was in shock this was a dream of mine come true. They had several pools, hot tubs, and lounge chairs all around the decks. I used the pool for my exercise and the hot tubs for my therapy. The heat felt so good and let's just say the jets in the hot tub were so strong. All you had to do was punch the button to restart them. How relaxing it was, all the nerves in my back felt at ease for a change. The sail was two days then to Bermuda. The name of the beach was Horseshoe Bay. The sand was light pink and beautiful it felt like walking on cotton so soft and fine. The water was so warm. We just went right in and stayed there for hours. It was turquoise blue, absolutely the best beach that I have ever seen in my entire life. Almost tranquil, no waves like the Jersey shore. Basking in the sun- you couldn't ask for anything better than that. The best way to describe it was breathtaking.

 The only thing I wished for was more time there. We had to be back on the ship by four. So onward we went. Time sure flew we got back onboard had to get ready for dinner. The next day I was up bright and early to catch the sunrise while I took pictures from my balcony. I never saw anything so beautiful then the sun reflecting on the water during early sunrise. This day was filled with shopping in San Juan, Puerto Rico. The streets were small, and they had all little businesses that tourists could buy souvenirs and plenty of tee shirts along with tons of key chains. It was a lot of walking, so I had to wear very comfy sneakers. They also have one of the largest diamond international stores around, very well known for diamonds. Speaking of diamonds, I went to a diamond seminar on board just in case someone wanted to purchase diamonds you were aware of the real ones versus the non-authentic ones. The most popular at the time was the Tanzanite diamond. A rare blue but very exquisite. As time passed so quickly, we had to get back, we walked so far out of the way we almost couldn't remember where the ship was. After a few blocks we came across the water then we knew we were getting closer to the dock. I was so nervous because I knew we were pressed for time, but we did make it back in time.

The next beach day was in St. Martin, I liked it. There wasn't my favorite spot but the best part of that was watching the eclipse with the paper glasses we were given the night before. It was something out of a picture, just beautiful. The sun and the moon together you; can't imagine seeing anything like it. Especially on a beach in broad daylight. Swimming also was a challenge because the waves were rough and it kept knocking you down. The funniest thing I ever saw was me and my friend standing there laughing and all of a sudden, we went down and we couldn't get up every time we tried to get up, we kept falling back in- it was hilarious. The time we get out of the water we want to get some sun and these ladies come waltzing over back and forth babbling, "Lady, do you want to buy something? How about a dress or a hat?" Now I'm like, "No, thanks." Five minutes later they are back again. I said, "Not interested." No less than ten minutes later, another one comes over. That's it. I pull out five dollars and say, "Give me that green hat." She replies, "Ten buck" I then say, "Five or go away." "Okay." I couldn't get a break, we just wanted to be in the sun and relax, it was my vacation. No patience for this kind of stuff. Other than that, the weather was beautiful we had a good day.

When we got to the last beach in Labadie, Haiti we somehow wound up on the wrong side, but it was great I loved it there. This was Royal Caribbean's resort. I'm talking hammocks tied to palm trees chairs set up for the tourists on this cruise, all for us. I felt like a VIP for a change. The cooks had an outdoor restaurant right there, they were cooking lunch for all of us who used this excursion. The best part of this was me and my friend sitting there at this picnic table eating like two queens laughing having a ball when I turned to her and said, "I'm going to write a book about this one day." She cracked up almost fell off the bench she said, "What about?" "Cruise therapy," I replied we laughed so hard I literally had tears rolling down my face. "Let me explain it's a great idea I'm going to go back home and tell my doctors that when they ask me what I did to get my back better or at least what did I do to relieve the pain I can tell them, 'Well doc, it all started like this... I decided that before I was going to go through heck because I knew what I was about to endure in the very near future I was going on a cruise. Lay in the sun to relax my brain, de-stress, swim in the pools for cold compresses on my back, then move over into a hot tub in about 102 degrees with jets to massage my muscles and the beach, to be knocked down by waves to give me the adjustments to get me into alignment as I keep tumbling over as the waves take me out flipping me over. The best part is coming back to put ice packs when I went to bed. Oh yeah, I had an awesome room attendant who took care of our room. I asked him if he can please give me an ice bucket each night filled with ice cubes to the top. Such a kind young man. That was the last of the excursions that we booked. However, we did get to see two Broadway shows in the theatre, one was a tribute to Queen called *We Will Rock You*. The other was a magic show, quite good and very entertaining. Along with that there was just so much to do such as nightclubs, all types of bars depending what kind of music a person chooses. We just liked walking alongside the desk at night and looking at the water. It was pitch black on the water all you could see is the reflection of the moon. You don't realize how far out in the Atlantic you are until you see if for yourself. All you can think of when you're looking out there is God made the oceans beautifully. It really does spread far, almost like it never ends.

I'm so happy that my friend and I had this opportunity to go on this cruise. It was the best vacation ever. Will never forget all the fun that I had especially on the swing by the pool made me feel just like a kid again. I am looking forward to going on another one God willing.

Now I was home at last from my nine days. It took a few days to regroup and relax and to get back into the swing of things. I knew my life was about to start changing because I still had to deal with the issue with my back and not feeling any better as far as the constant pain I was in, and I needed to do something because deep in my heart I knew that I wasn't going to be able to go back to work anytime soon. A few months later my short-term disability was going to end, and I wouldn't be getting paid anymore from my prior job, so I contacted an attorney to try to see if I had a case for social security disability. The appointment was made and all set to go. The lawyer had me sign a contract on October

24th, 2017, and said, "I am going to take on your case. However, I do need you to get a few tests for me." So, I had to go for a nerve conduction test along with an MRI. I had a problem with getting the MRI approved. I even had to go to an orthopedic doctor along with my pain management doctor. They fought for me with my insurance and three months later I was able to be tested. During this time had a primary care physician who decided that after he gave me a signed doctor not for me to go on temporary disability, he refused to sign anymore paperwork for me. This became a living nightmare for me. He was very reluctant to do anything for me, which I thought was very unprofessional. I had no choice but to change physicians.

    I really started praying to Jesus for His guidance because I didn't know what was happening or where to go from there, I just knew I had to listen to what my attorney suggested that I do and of course listen to the Holy Spirit inside me to calm me down. I started to get frantic because after the application was filled out it took some time to hear back, I was officially denied in writing. I said to myself, "Oh my God, now what should I do?" I was so upset that we had to make an appeal with social security in writing and there went another year. This started when I was working in a retail store and the last day, I worked at was July 17, 2017. One night, I was lying in bed, not able to sleep, twisting and turning also praying for help and I heard the Lord speak to me softly. He said to me, "Child, this is going to be one of the biggest steps of faith that you will ever go through, and it's going to be the hardest things you will endure but you must trust in me." I said, "Okay, I will." So much time passed, I waited and waited for a court date. Finally, I received the letter with the set court date.

I went to court and my attorney spoke a little to the judge then the judge gave him the platform, so my lawyer asked me a bunch of questions in which I answered. I was nervous because when I left there with no answer. I couldn't believe this just happened. I went home and I cried and cried. I was so confused and had knots in my stomach. A few months later, I got the call from my lawyer that the judge couldn't make his mind up if he wanted to give it to me or not. He was truly undecided and that I may have to go back to court. Now I really can't deal with all this. My stress levels are literally through the roof, so I started to go to counseling. I spoke to my friend, and she even noticed that I was having some trouble with this process. I was getting very depressed and having lots of anxiety attacks. I had to get counseled each week along with going to physical therapy.

So, I had to wait again because there was going to be another court date which was February 6, 2020. But this time we showed up at the courthouse and my lawyer had a problem hearing the judge because he was on a plane the day before and was jet lagged and had a hearing issue. Each time the judge asked a question his response was, "I can't hear you." Anyway, I had to state my name and swear to tell the truth and raise my right hand on the Bible. We proceeded the judge wanted me to give my testimony, so I did I went on to tell him about the herniated discs and the sciatica nerves that run down both of my legs causing my feet to go numb and my back burning like it was on fire, along with the tingling and pins and needles down my legs all the time. I told him I couldn't stand for more than an hour and I couldn't sit for more than a half hour to hour without pain. The clerk was like the devil on my right side telling the court of jobs that she felt I could do right after I spoke. I truly gave it my all; 100% of truth went into my verbal statement. My attorney started arguing with the judge about something which made no sense to do. I felt as if he totally blew it for me. So, here I am again in the same situation as before with appealing it again, in April 2020. I thought to myself, *What now? God, I cannot even believe all this is happening to me why? Now I need you to help me.* This became my prayer day and night seven days a week. Constantly making requests known before the Lord. Crying in the middle of the night, not being able to sleep, having so much anxiety and depression in a loss for words. I really thought this would have been done and over by now. I was so frustrated with this process words cannot even begin to express how I was feeling. No job, no money coming in at all. Until one day I was in my room quietly when I turned on my computer and did some research on how I could get some financial help or something when I came across the application for a SNAP card and general assistance from the government.

I tried to get the application to submit for about three hours and it just wouldn't go through. I went downstairs to have dinner and when I came back upstairs back to my PC it went through. *Like a miracle*, I thought. Thank Jesus for that small favor. I was sent a letter in the mail for me to go see social services, and that I would be assigned to a case worker regarding my application to get food and cash. This, too, wasn't that easy of course. I had to get all the documentation to prove my case and I did just that. One month later I got the SNAP card so that I could buy food along with some cash assistance because I had no income, not even temporary disability. Again, God shows up to provide for me just like He promised in his word. (Philippians 4:12). Somehow, He always knew what I needed before I asked.

Once again, I was denied. Now, we appealed the decision. I had to get more medical documents on top of my whole file already because it's going to make my case stronger, so I started counseling in 2017. I was seeing a therapist for about a year then I moved to a different facility where the staff had a physiatrist on board. I needed to get some files sent to my attorney's office with an updated letter which stated I cannot work. They refused to help me. They wouldn't even return any of my attorney's phone calls on several occasions. They had tried to reach out to this facility and were totally ignored. I left there and went elsewhere, to the place where I am now. I was seen by a whole new group of doctors and I liked it there. My therapist is very nice and understanding about what I was going through. When I needed letters for my case to give to my attorney, they were more than happy to help me. My appeal was being held with the appeals council in Virginia since April 2020. I am awaiting the final decision for the appeal. It has been four years of battle.

When you are going through something in life as per say a "storm" it's so easy to lose focus because your attention is always on the waves and the rocks that are hitting you from all different directions. It's so important not to lose perspective on the fact that storms never last forever and Jesus always finds a way to calm the storm when it gets to be more than you can handle. I've learned that with this journey of life that I was and am still on. Try to remember all your hopes comes from God. To hope in Him and through Him. To have faith that's unmovable and unshakable in while waiting an answer to prayers. Some may take longer time than others, but they do all get answered. We just need to be patient and wait upon the Lord, that's when our strength is renewed. (Isaiah 40:31). The most important thing is to have trust in the Lord. (Proverbs 3:5-6).

Chapter 3

The world was in total shutdown due to the Covid-19 virus that struck us in March 2020. We were in a lockdown for six months. The pandemic that no one ever expected or even knew how to address it. I lost a close girlfriend of mine for many years. She went into the hospital and never came out. Life just has not been the same ever since. My dear friend you will always remain in my heart and truly be missed. Just a small dedication I'd like to add a tribute in loving memory. Dealing with loss isn't easy but I know that one fine day I will see her again in heaven. God promised to wipe our tears away He gathers them in a bottle to give back to us. (Psalms 56:8). We all deal with different types of loss, maybe through a loved one that passed or a broken relationship or something worse and we all grieve and it's totally okay to let out those feelings and emotions. This is why we need to fix our eyes on the one true God who holds our future in His hands and be thankful each day for His blessing. Not only accept His blessing but to be a blessing to someone else who may be going through something.

I have had more than my share of trials and tribulation while on this journey of life. Which makes me so happy to know that I have a God who causes me to persevere always. I thank JESUS for what He did for me with His mercy alone and giving me the grace even when I didn't deserve it, He gives it regardless of the situation. When I was a little girl, only three years old, my dad left. Although I was too young; I do remember the absence of him not being with me or there which caused me so much pain and I felt abandoned and didn't know who to turn to because none of my childhood friends would know what this was like for me. When I was seven, there are certain things I still can remember like when my mom told me that my dad was coming to pick me up to take me out for my birthday, so she put a pretty dress on me with my black shoes and I was standing outside of my house waiting and waiting noticing that it's been more than an hour and dad was a complete no show. Soon enough I'd run right back in the house yelling and screaming because I was so upset and disappointed. I don't recall a lot of things but some I can still like it was just yesterday. As time passed, your sense of security lessens and you may have trust issues. We all pretty much do it in some sort of way, but we move on. I've learned to live, love, and let go. But the memory is part of the past that doesn't just erase itself.

Having the knowledge of a loving Heavenly Father and His compassion makes it so much easier to deal with forgiveness. Because of the goodness of God's mercy. I count all lost because nothing can compare.

It turned to autumn. All the trees were changing colors and you could feel a chill in the air. It felt like it was just summer not too long ago and time kept moving. We were on a worldwide lockdown which meant the courts were still closed therefore my appeal hadn't come up yet. Time just slowed it down even more but I hoped that this will all be resolved very soon. The last time I spoke to my attorney was in July 2020 she had mentioned that they are waiting for an analyst to review my file and case. All I could do was keep praying for approval at this level.

On another note, I started taking Bible classes every Wednesday night at my church. Because we still weren't having services except online, I still felt the need to go in and spend some alone time with God to pray.

It's like a release for me mentally, it helps me and gives me so much hope. I always loved being in the house of the Lord. Since I was very young. I always had a desire to know about Jesus. Something nice happened the day I made my communion, I walked into the church with all the other children in my class and we all were told to form two lines boys and girls and when I sat down it just so happened that I was chosen to walk the chalice up to the priest on my special day. I felt as if God had chosen me for that and I knew He had a calling on my life. Shortly after that I told my mom that, "I quit going to the Catholic Church because I didn't feel it was for me." That was when my mom and I started going a Christian church where I could learn and grow up spiritually. Soon enough I was singing in the choir, and I became a member of the congregation. I loved the pastor there because he had a real heart for God. He sometimes would come to my house to visit my family all the time just to pray with us. Not only that he was very giving I still remember I wanted to go on a youth retreat to Pennsylvania for the weekend but couldn't afford to go and the pastor came over and gave my mom money for me to go. I was so happy and grateful, not to mention I had a great time. Some people may say how can you have a good time in church? My childhood friends used to say that to me all the time. I used to tell them I have a ball there, it's awesome why don't you come with me sometime? But their parents wouldn't allow them to come with me, I never knew why. There is a song lyric I heard once that fits this description, "though none go with me still I will follow, the cross before me the world behind me.". That's basically how I live my life.

As I got into my twenties I started working out because I wanted to get in shape and take care of myself. So, I made the commitment to exercise from then on. Weight loss has always been a challenge for me because I love food but then again who doesn't? I was always up and down with weight, but I had to learn about nutrition. I'm very experienced with the gym industry just by being in the fitness industry. I enjoyed it very much. All my successes started there. I really feel that I've accomplished more than I ever wanted but there will always be something else to learn about. Some of my other passions include traveling, cooking, and cosmetics. Growing up Italian, I've learned to cook because I would always be in the kitchen with mom, so she taught me everything I know. I plan to travel soon. I really enjoy it whether it be flying somewhere for cruising, but these are just some of my dreams. I would like the opportunity to see Greece and the Caribbean again. I know that God has a plan for me as for all who love Him it says it in His word. (Jeremiah 29:11). I'd trade my plans for His plans anytime because He wants the best for me, and He knows what is best for me. All He asks us, is to trust him and he will give us the desires of our hearts.

We all make choices in life, and we are given the chance to live a life of abundance according to the word of God however this only applies you are in His will for your life this doesn't mean that you should go out and do all things unpleasing to Him or so be it have it your way because that doesn't work. This is why He says that His thoughts are so much higher than our thoughts and what we may think is good is not good not only that but if you're not in His will daily by reading and praying and spending time with God your life can wind up a disaster just like the prodigal son who squandered all he had until he went broke and came home to his father. If he only had stayed where he was from the beginning, he wouldn't have made a mess of his life only to return home. The human race, no matter what denomination you come from, and what so-called religion you may or may not be, we need to return to God. Meaning be humble and admit you're a sinner. We all come short of the glory of God. It's only by His grace that we can be saved.

Getting back to the lockdown and being not able to go out like before, caused us to self-reflect on our own lives and get our hearts right with God. We are certainly living near the end times as per Bible prophecy. The book of Revelation, speaks about certain things that will occur in the heavens and on earth. Just to give some examples of earthquakes, fire, whether changes meaning not knowing what season we will be in climate changes, locusts, plagues, more deaths and murders. It also speaks of the sounding of the trumpets so we must be ready for the second coming of Christ. Be as a watchman at night because no one will know exactly the hour or day because He will come like a thief in the night also in the twinkling of an eye.

I would like to have the opportunity to have everything go back to normal again. For example, my closest friend had to move away because she simply couldn't afford to live in the metropolitan area due to rents being so expensive, so she moved down south toward the shore area. This has been hard for me, too, because we were there for each other every day and saw each other all the time. But everyone moves on at some point. Ever wonder why certain people come into your life at certain times? Some are there for years and some for a few months. Sometimes, it's hard to accept that people must live their own lifestyle and do what is right for them.

I personally don't have lots of friends, but I know a lot of people through the years just from working in different places throughout my lifetime. Now that I have been trying so hard to deal with not working anymore it's very difficult for me because I don't see many people that much anymore accept when I'm at my gym. I have a lot of acquaintances now. Since this virus started my appeal for my SSDI has been postponed or held back until the courts open and this is why I am extremely frustrated. This whole process is very complicated for anyone to go through. I think that it shouldn't have never happened like the way that it did for me. I have all the documents and letters from doctors that I can get and have done everything in my power that I can. I just must wait. I really hope this turns out in my favor because of this pandemic situation. Being stressed at times and feeling so discouraged by this is tiring I'm so exhausted mentally and physically sick due to this. This is how this process has made me feel and I honestly will be so happy when it's over and done. Stamped, approved, signed, sealed, and delivered. I must hang in there and be still. This is weighing on me because not having any income and worrying how I'm going to pay my bills due to my money in the bank being drained out. I cry out to Jesus all the time for His provision to provide me with financial blessings.

Some of the worst things that I started to feel was that I wished that I was well enough where I wouldn't have had to even apply for disability benefits because if I knew then what I know now, I wouldn't of even went to see an attorney. But then again, I somehow knew Jesus would turn this all around for His glory. When you're in a circumstance it's hard to see what's ahead because you're in it, however this is why you shouldn't focus on the problem but on God and what His promise was to me. Trust, Faith, Be Still and Know that I am God. (Psalms 46:10, NKJV). Those were the kind of thoughts I had going through this process not only in my thoughts but in my prayer book as well. I've written several prayers at the time when I was really depressed and needed to sit and pray. Sometimes, it's good to have a close friend to talk to but when no one is around I would pull out my journal and just write it kept me calmer after doing so.

To get back to reality, our focus shouldn't be on worldly events that happen day to day but try to think of more positive things. I am not trying to say that being a Christian makes everything peaches and cream and that none of us will have problems because it's not, and although most people don't like to talk about depression. But I'm here to say that it's does exist to some extent. Let me explain so you can understand, a person can be in a current environment or situation and not be happy with the place they are in and that makes them very uncomfortable and irritable or even miserable and following that comes the feeling of being depressed and overwhelmed with certain things that happen over a period can also do it too. Especially, if you didn't really let it go, this is why talk therapy is good. It gets you to talk about the things that in secret really bother you. I'm sure at some point we will all go through this in one form or another. The pandemic has everyone's attention now no one knows for sure what the future will be like with most things' shutdown. We, as a people, don't like being tied down or held back for any reason but we must be cautious about distancing ourselves to avoid getting this virus. Stress levels are on a high time high right now. I'm looking forward to seeing things the way they were but what if this is the new normal? Will we all be able to accept it? I feel that the churches should be open for regular services but that goes against social distancing but keeping the bars and beaches open is, okay? Double standard or a political move? Think about it… Surprisingly, at a time when we need God more than ever and we need to be hearing from him every day in our walk just because the church wasn't having inside person services doesn't mean we don't find a room in our house to pray in.

Fall arrives and leaves on trees change colors and they fall to the ground. Then winter comes bringing white snow to make the trees look especially on the branches where the leaves once were. Then we look for spring flowers to bloom then back to summertime heat. Even the earth goes through a process of change, and it had no choice but to accept it. It's all about routine for life that needs change and sometimes change is good.

I am not one who likes things to always stay the same, I don't have a problem with change. It's called growing. You also can grow spiritually if you like change because it shows that you're teachable or willing to learn and go further in your daily walk with the Lord. Each morning when I get up and make my coffee I sit down and just say, "Thank you, Jesus." I'm very thankful for everything He has done for me. It's important to me that I let Him know and that I appreciate what He has done for me. Then I begin my prayers. In my imagination, I always think that in heaven there are many gift boxes with blessings in them and all we must do is reach heaven and just pull the blessings down from heaven to earth. The reason why I think like this is because I know that all of what we need is already there waiting for us to believe that it does exist. If Jesus said, "In my house are many mansions and I go and prepare a place for you," then why wouldn't everything else be just as he described? (John 14:2).

The fact is that there is a real heaven just as hell is also very real or the Bible would have no mention of it. If someone were to ask me, "What if all this is just a fairy tale or perhaps just a story?" Would that persuade you into thinking we were all wrong? My reply would be, "I'd rather believe in that it is all truth then not to believe and find out when I get to heaven that I was right." I rather not take that chance at compromising what my belief systems are. You must have an unshakable faith in the heavenly realm and all things of heaven. Don't be moved for any reason or let anything shake you up into thinking opposite of your belief. Hold fast onto that which things are all created by Him and through Him. Including the heavens and the earth. Most of the time you will be put into a situation where you may think there is no way out of the mess and you become all too involved with the exterior of the problem the best way for anyone who is in this would be to say to God, "Change my perspective or the lens in which I am seeing this through help me to see it through your eyes." See if you only can look through a lens that's not focused correctly you won't be able to see clearly the whole thing or the whole picture unless you adjust the lens. What I mean by that is don't look at the problem look to Jesus in all His glory because He is the beginning, middle, and the end. No matter how hard or how long it takes He knows the past, present, and future of your whole life story. Keep your eyes fixed on the cross.

There have been so many times when I wanted to just throw in the towel and give up. Time after time I'd ask myself is this all worth it. I've gotten so discouraged that drove me to having panic attacks. Not even to mention the sleepless nights that would go on for the past few years. Everywhere I went and anyone who had gone through anything like this I would ask them what they did, and you know they all said the same thing. Patience takes a long time; you have to just be able to wait. Well, we know how we all want things in a snap just like that, but life doesn't work like that unfortunately. What's the cliché "good things come to those who wait." It started to make sense to me when I was reading the Word, and I came across the verse, "Those who wait upon the Lord will renew their strength." (Isaiah 40:31). That's when I knew in my heart, I had no choice but to wait no surrender it totally and fully to God.

It was on October 28, 2020 I was sitting in the kitchen and something said to me *call up social security office to see how far along my case was*, so I did just that and the gentlemen I spoke to was very nice on the phone he advised me that it's been about six months' time which was something like 230 days after the date I appealed April 1, 2020. He informed me that they are working on my case file, and I should hear back soon and that it's moving along. Now I have been praying for God's speed on this and I know that three years is longer than I had expected, but I trusted in God for breakthrough to come and come soon I just want this to be over so I can move on with my life. I needed to have an income just to pay my bills. I am so tired of not having any income coming in and I cannot live like this any longer, so I pleaded and cried out to Jesus to help me. I will await the letter with the final decision of the counsel in Virginia. I'm expecting an approval in Jesus's name.

When I say I cried out to Jesus, I really do mean it I shed more tears over this situation than over anything else in a long time. I know He will be my great defender and mighty in council. This is the finish line; I'm running the race that was set before me and the devil will not win this battle. This battle belongs to the Lord. Sometimes, when you get into a disagreement or an argument with someone you already know or a loved one for whatever reason it can be very easily taken care of but when you're fighting with the courts and their systems it's a whole different thing. It gets to the point where there is nothing you can do but wait. But while you are waiting you serve the Lord. Go to church when you can, seek His face daily, read the word, worship, sing, and praise Him evermore because it's what he deserves no matter what 'storm' in life you go through. "Praise Him in the Storm" was a song written by Casting Crowns that brought me so much encouragement beyond anything I ever heard it just hit me in such a way to exactly where I was in my life during that time. I have such a desire for music ministry that I cannot wait until I can fulfill my true calling to get involved. I honestly feel that I am in the right place where I should be, and I do not plan on moving. My feet are planted on a firm foundation, and I love the church that I attend. I look forward to when I can sing again but I must be led to the specific time which is when the Holy Spirit guides me to do so. Only then will I make a move. When you feel "led" this means that the Holy Spirit inside you starts tugging in your heart pushing you to do something in the right direction toward the things of God you will know. You also must be able to hear Gods voice when He does speak to your heart. It's that still quiet voice that gently whispers to you then you will know only if you're paying attention. The Bible speaks very clear that Jesus states My sheep hear my voice". (John10:27).

Often someone may ask me how do you know what the things of God are I'm a good person doesn't that count? My reply would always be "being a good person to who? People?" My opinion is this, whatever things are true, whatever things are noble, whatever things are just, whatever things are pure, whatever things are lovely, whatever things are of good report, if there is any virtue and if there is anything praiseworthy—meditate on these things. (Philippians 4:8).

You cannot get into heaven by your own merits its only through the shedding of the blood of Jesus that you may bring yourself to repentance for the forgiveness of sins. That is Salvation. So many people are so misinformed about the fact that they think just by being a Good Samaritan that would be enough, but the truth is it's not true. It's simple it's what you have done for God that matters?

Are you after His heart and earnestly seeking to know Him? Are you also willing to follow Him by turning away from your ways to follow in His footsteps? When I was just sixteen years old in high school, we had to do an essay to write. I wrote about what it meant to me to be a Christian and I would like to share that to my readers. I hope that it will inspire you and touch your heart… I must go in my attic to get it and bring it here so that I can retype it.

This is the real copy, word for word, of that essay.

> The one most important thing that ever happened to me was when I became a Christian. What that simply means is when a person accepts Jesus Christ in their life as their personal Lord of their life. As a Christian, you must be baptized in the Holy Spirit. The Holy Spirit is when you receive the Heavenly language, which is known as Tongues. You also receive other gifts such as Wisdom and Knowledge to read and understand the Bible. You also must be water baptized in the water and by doing that the pastor of the church prays over you and you go under water which states your sins are washed away. Being a Christian I've experienced a lot of joy, peace, and love within myself. What I enjoy about being a Christian is that when you become a born again. Your life is planned out for your future and your life is straight. I am limited certain things in life, and one is to serve God every day in my Christian daily walk.
>
> Jodi A. Luberto
Age 16
November 7th, 1984

Chapter 4

The fact is that I have always wanted to do more in my life than I did but because I've always worked since I was thirteen years old. I have not had much time to travel. I would love to travel soon, hopefully things get better by next year. 2020 has not been a good one since the lockdown in March till August. My plan is to go back on another cruise and go to Florida to visit my good friends. Life does have its twists and turns as we know it. Stay strong and stay encouraged for the most part. I think of it this way when you are at a high time low things can only go up from there. Nothing ever stays the same just like the seasons.

It's always been my dream to go back to Cancun, Mexico again or even see more of those islands. I dream of having my very own apartment one day soon. I have been through a lot of disappointments already and now I'm ready for a breakthrough. I am so ready to receive my miracle that I have been praying for the past few years. I truly think that I have made all my requests to Jesus and have totally surrendered them all in His hands. I choose to let Him fight my battles for me now. I will continue to fight my battles in prayer with the faith believing that all will come to pass. I know in my heart that the Lord sees and hears everything, even the things we don't say. There are so many times where I just don't know exactly what else to pray for because I honestly feel that I have opened my heart up to Him so much that I ran out of words. I also know that God knows what we all need and that He provides each time. I thank God for all the times where I needed a job, He was right there to give me one. Time and time again. He provided for me when I thought there was no way and in a matter of weeks He'd come through. I always will be grateful for leading me and guiding me to this point. Although I don't know the outcome, I do know in His time it all works out.

Now into the holiday season soon it will be Christmas of 2020 although it hardly seems like it or even feels like it because of all the turmoil of this pandemic. I try each and every day to rise above it by telling myself that if I woke up and have air in my lungs today it's a good day. I try too always find the good in things even in bad situations. I am not confrontational at all unless someone gets in my face about an issue then I will be straight forward with that person or persons on a civilized level, however there are times that I just rather keep my mouth shut and keep walking. I have a lot of tolerance but once I get to that final breaking point then I will speak my mind. Too me it's about keeping the peace and my sanity which is more valuable, but people today are nasty and have bad attitudes toward one another, at a time of the year we are and should all come together and Worship the King Jesus.

I can think of what Jesus said on the cross, "Forgive them because they do not know what they do." That must be the most honest thing ever said in all history. We all do things that we have no idea what we are doing. The way we treat our own family or friends and even strangers, the disrespect or regard to anyone's feelings. In this world we live in, humans conduct is terrible on all levels. The thing that boggles my mind is that this is just a stomping ground or pit stop until God calls us home. If people cannot get along here, how are they going to get along in heaven? There is no diversion in the Heavens and no fighting. I tend to think "when is enough already?" We still must pray for the Salvation for the unsaved regardless of what they do to you. I'm not saying to be a doormat and let anyone mistreat or abuse you in any way. Say a simple prayer give it to Jesus let Him take care of the rest.

I wrote this book because if it helps just one person who can relate and agree with me then I have done a good thing. I truly give God all the glory. I hope it also brings light to your world as we are the salt and light of the world. A hope that you never knew exists. But it does. His name is Jesus. He is a way maker and a promise keeper miracle worker. I will always praise His name because He is worthy of all my praise. We should give Him an offering of praise for all He has done for us.

There is a song that was written for Christmas time, the lyrics are "We bring an offering of worship to our King. No one on earth deserves the praises that we sing, Jesus, may you receive the honor that you're due. Lord, we bring an offering to you." This was just one of those songs that hits your heart every time you hear it. It moved me so much.

This year 2020 was a very tough year I think for everyone. No one ever expected the country to even come close to a lockdown and a virus that contaminated thousands of people all at once and took the lives of many. I have seriously felt the pain and discomfort of this on another level. Being that all the government agencies were still closed; the courts were very much closed, which meant my appeals court is closed, and I had to keep waiting until they opened back up. Unless they were working from home. I called the social security office in Washington, D.C. and spoke to someone that did in fact tell me someone is working on my disability case and that I should be hearing from them soon. So, in good faith I'm trusting in Jesus to pull me through this. This process was harder than I thought. If anyone must go and try for disability, I'd like to advise one thing, make sure your lawyer is a good one. Take my advice on this. I have been waiting three years now. Seems like this waiting process takes way too long for anyone to bear.

Most days, I'm going over this in my head I hope it gets approved and not denied again. I cannot handle another denial. I literally feel like I'm going to have a mental breakdown at times getting myself sick inside. Having no income for three years and nothing to live on but food stamps, it's impossible for anyone to have a normal life. I cannot even go into a clothing store and buy anything unless I use a credit card, but how will I pay that with a credit card when the bill comes in the mail?

Time after time I've wanted to just go shopping for myself and I can't do that because I must watch every dime I have now in my bank account. I must pay for my car insurance, phone, medical bill along with my credit card bill from a few months ago. In my head I keep saying, "It will all be over soon. I will somehow, someway win this case." But then it feels like I'm going to be wrapped up in this for a long time again. Every time I try to avoid this thought I cannot stop the thought from entering my head again and again. I am so drained mentally and physically from this whole entire situation. This is what I went through daily. Up against the wall with no room to move! Plain out stuck in a rut. After a while of having the pity party in my mind the blinders start to come off and then.

I remember, *ah where does my real help come from?* I know more than anyone it comes from the Lord. I know this so I should know better, however I am only human, and I am not invincible I hurt just like everyone else. Being Christian doesn't at all mean that we don't feel disappointment at times in life. There may even be times when we just want to scream or cry and that's all okay too, it's because we have a conscience. Just a few examples: When someone is being treated in a certain way by someone and all of a sudden, this person disappoints you, we feel that separation right away. There are going to be times when you think a person is your friend until you find out that they have moved on with their lives and forgot all about you. Which causes you to question, "Were they really a true friend?"

This can be very hurtful to a person. So, we all at some points have been through this or something on this level or worse. The thing is this what do we do when we come across this? Do we become a doormat for anyone to walk on us? How do we cope with certain individuals? How do we keep the Christian principles in line without the confrontations? Just implement a resolve without stirring the pot for a potential argument. Yet still be loving or do it in love?

The thing is this, there isn't a person in the world who likes being taken advantage of by another person. Most out there will always mistake kindness for weakness. Meaning you may be the nicest person with a heart of gold and there will always be that one person that will most likely think you're weak. I have personally met these types of people often in the past and present. So, it takes a very patient individual to get to the point where you need to nip this in the bud before it gets out of hand, because if you don't it can escalate. You are not weak; you are strong and too intelligent to let this go on any further. Defiantly confront the issue with the person or people and set them straight. I have recently had to make some very strong decisions regarding this myself and said, "No more I'm finished with giving when I simply cannot afford to give what I don't have." Honesty is always best said than avoiding the issues.

Dealing with people takes patience that's where we need to seek God for that in our prayer life. "Lord, teach us your patience." Just a simple prayer like that will make a difference in the weeks ahead. I have been through this several times in my life when I wanted to get into heated arguments but at the last minute, I've just decided to keep quiet and not entertain the thought of fighting back and wasting my energy. I was at that point, and I had to give it to God and let Him be my defender. Let Him fight my battles.

The day finally arrived when I opened my email and saw the mail that will be coming on December 7, 2020. So, quickly I ran to the mailbox and the letter from social security in Virginia was there, I tore open the letter with so much anticipation and nervousness to read. *Denied* again. I said as the tears then started rolling down my cheeks. I was in total shock I just couldn't believe this happened to me again. Last night at 10:30 p.m. I sent my attorney a simple email asking if they heard anything yet? I then got an email in the afternoon stating that I am no longer being represented anymore by this office. Which was totally fine with me, because prior to the last appeal I had advised them that I will be seeking another attorney to handle my case if this goes sour. Well, it did! I'm devastated. So, what do I do? I got in touch with plan B which was another lawyer. We spoke briefly then I had to fax a letter which I had received from my psychiatrist a few months ago to her office. In response to this conversation, I was informed that she would look it over and if she sees fit, she will call me. The next day, December 8, 2020, she called and scheduled another appointment with me to gather all the information she needs for December 21, 2020. She will be now representing me with a new claim for SSDI benefits.

As far as everything else, now my ban at the product testing facility was lifted. I just started a back patch for two weeks which will pay me a few hundred dollars. Last year I was doing product testing for two different places, and I got in trouble, so I was banned for one year. Unfortunately, when I was testing, I was finished with the one place but didn't give it a few days to rest before getting onto another test and they saw the medical marker dots and questioned me about it. So that was what had happened, which led to the ban. I learned my lesson with that.

I had my psychiatrist appointment and we discussed my medications. We lowered the dosage on the antidepressant to a lower mg. Because when I take the higher mg I sweat very badly. He thinks it can be a reaction to the medicine that causes sweating profusely. I know I'm going through menopause very badly, but this was different, and I had a hard time thinking this has such severity of nonstop sweats. I also explained how I have been feeling from not sleeping at night and feeling miserable to even feeling off and very stressed out along with feeling depressed. This is real for me. It's a real problem and many people really do have this. The best way to describe it is that one minute I can be fine, the next I'm crying day and night. Feeling hopelessness and like nothing ever works out for me in my life. This time of year, is hard for me. I have so many emotions that get all out of whack. I wish I felt better. So, what does this mean for me? Well, basically because I was again denied my SSDI, we will be filling out a new file application and starting over as well as giving all new information. I'm not sure how this is all going to work so I had to get all my paperwork together from my personal files. The thing is now that I am very overwhelmed with the way that this whole ordeal went down. This should never have happened like this. I can only conclude that my previous attorney was a lazy person, and he yanked my chain for the past three years, causing me to get rid of him and go elsewhere after all the hard work that I have done to get all the doctor's medical records from each doctor who treated me.

How do I just forget the past three years and move on from this? I'm all out of energy and don't have the fight in me now to do anything. This is where it got hard for me to accept, but I have absolutely no choice in the matter. I just know that I must keep fighting this until I win. There is no way I can go back working. My back hurts even for me to stand up for an hour straight. The only thing I can do is give this new lawyer a chance at getting this for me. Believe me, I wished it was all over but it wasn't. At least not yet. This is the tough part. To keep my faith and trust in the Lord. I know my patience is running thin and I needed more patience to pursue this again. I'm became really upset because it was Christmas time and I was hoping for a better outcome than this. If you were me, what would you do? Give up or keep fighting? I really didn't feel that this battle is mine anymore. I need to give this one over to God and let Him deal with this. I keep saying, "Maybe one day

I will get to go to Florida to visit my friends as soon as this is all over." It's been three years and I still haven't had the opportunity or the money to go anywhere. I'm not sure how to get money but I just know I need money to pay my bills for the upcoming year. I feel that I have the right to ask Jesus why didn't this go in my favor? Aren't I loved enough? I am seriously a wreck, and even more emotional now. Just because we may be Christian doesn't necessarily mean that we won't have problems that are too much for us to bear on our own. The even says that we will walk through fire and waters, but we will not burn or drown because Jesus is there to catch us when we do. I honestly think that it's all perseverance that causes us to get to the other side or, shall I say, through the tunnel. What I mean by the "tunnel" is that sometimes we find ourselves in a huge tunnel with light at the end of it. However, we cannot see what's on the other end of the tunnel because we are right in the middle of it. We just know that there is a bright light at the end of it. The key to getting to the end is to keep being persistent. I know that this is not easy at all. No matter what you may be facing today or even what may be lurking around the corner, know that God is always behind the scenes working on our behalf. I believe this with all my heart. I also should know better by now that all things that happen aren't always the devil. Remember that I've said that a "delay" will serve its purpose.

A perfect example for this would be in Ecclesiastes (3:3) where it clearly states "Everything has its time." The purpose under Heaven. There is nothing that God doesn't know. He knows our pains and struggles. There isn't a sin He doesn't already know. Just be truthful with Him. I do this myself. I wouldn't have made it this far if I didn't have understanding on his Love for me. I have been so disappointed over and over because things didn't go the way that I wanted things to go and I've been brought down to my knees many times, but that's when I ask myself who is the pilot here, me or God? If I really gave my problem to Him and let it go completely then why do I get upset and want to take it back from his hands? When I gave it to Him in the first place. Then that would be a conflict on my part then how can I expect Him to do His thing for me, and work on my behalf?

The fact remains that I still have to trust in the Lord in every area of my life. I'm going to be the first one to admit it's very difficult to get used to disappointment and although we don't understand why certain things happen like they do, but they do happen, so they had to happen. It's all part of the plan. One Bible verse that gets me through every trial and tribulation is Jeremiah (29:11). I would read this repeatedly. That states, "I know the plans I have for you, plans to prosper you and not to harm you, and to give you a future." We all need to trust that Jesus wants nothing more than to provide us with good things and a hopeful future in Him. He does want to see His children prosper. He wants us to have a good life in Him. That is why we call Him a Good Father. He is the Father to the fatherless, a father to the orphan. He truly wants good for us.

Chapter 5

I was listening to the radio, and I heard this song that I have not heard in many years, and it literally brought tears to my eyes. The name of the song was called, "Thank You." by Ray Boltz. It speaks about a pastor who taught Sunday school and when this child was only eight years old and heard the word of God being preached, he asked Jesus in his heart, and that he has a life that was changed by His generosity. I couldn't help but remember my Pastor of the church I got saved in this song was a perfect song for me. Who would think that many years later you can be so moved by a Christian artist that it literally brings you back to that time? I personally would like to thank that pastor for giving his life to do the work of the Lord, because I wouldn't have been saved if it wasn't for Him. He has gone home to be with the Lord. I would like to acknowledge him in this moment.

There were so many people who impacted my life as a child that they are no longer around nowadays. I will not forget them, because they truly helped me along the way in my personal walk with the Lord. Everyone needs Christian friends to encourage you when things aren't going to good. I haven't had many true Christian friends myself as I got older and the older, I get it just seems harder to find good people out there, so I spent a lot of time by myself maturing in God. Now I choose my friend wisely so not to be in bad company.

People try to persuade you into thinking that their way is the right way, but I just stick to what I know and have been taught in the church. One God, one way. The Holy Trinity is the only way I believe and there is no compromise. Father, Son, and Holy Spirit are three in one. Jesus. Although this may be difficult to explain or understand for some, we aren't supposed to understand it completely because it goes much deeper than we would be able to comprehend.

I read in an article it's like this: H2O is water. It can be an ice cube, hot water to room temperature water, at different times. However, it is still water. Many people from all religions simply all have their own ideas on if Jesus is the one and only Messiah. I do feel that everyone who doesn't want to accept Jesus for being the one true God is in for a rude awakening in the second coming of Christ. Then everyone who hasn't believed will then see for themselves. One morning, I was sitting in my kitchen, and I started to have my prayer session with Jesus and as I closed my eyes, I began that prayer and this is what was included in that prayer. I began to pray,

Dear God; I thank you for giving us your Son who laid His life down for my life to give me your mercy and your forgiveness for the sins that I came short of and that you took upon yourself my sins and you were nailed to a cross, and you took my place and did that just for me. There isn't enough praise that I can give you for all that you have done for me. There isn't enough worship that I can do for all you have given me. I thank you for your provision in all that you provided for me. Lord, I pray for this world and our nation that this is OUR time now.

We, as Christians, need to take a stand for America to humble ourselves and pray for God to turn this around and to move mountains in the situation that our governments now in. I pray that they will put God back in America again. I also pray that our government will realize that they have no power because they have a high seat or a title. No one has the power you have they are nothing for everything that they have you gave to them. Lord, I pray for them to fall to their knees and recognize who you are and return to you and repent for the selfishness and greed. Bring them to repentance, because you sit high above the heavens and watch over the earth, and you are in control over it all. Amen.

As we are a chosen generation which is what we are seeing now and soon. Now during this time of uncertainty, we need to decide who we are going to follow? Because tomorrow isn't guaranteed for anyone of us. Do not be ignorant to the truth found in God's Word. Let your heart be your guide to finding real peace and real joy not as the world gives but of the One true God. He reigns above all the heavens and the earth. He knows all knowing, and He knows the past, present and the future of every person. He chose this generation to see the revelations of the end times revealed and we are right in the middle of it all. It's all starting to unfold as He said it would. Kings and kingdoms will all pass away. Nations against nations. The economics of this world are starting to crumble with no stability anymore, people just living for themselves and not showing love to one another. The list goes on and on. It must change us as a human race must change our selfish ways and our carnal thinking. We need to bow down before the throne of God and connect with Him daily. We don't want to miss His second return which will be soon ready be watching and most of all be steadfast in our prayer life because when we hear the trumpet sound, we will then know that our Savior has come.

Christmas that year for me was challenging because I had several conflicting things that, let's just say, I had to decide what type of person I wanted to be, or the person Jesus would want me to be. It's like I had mentioned earlier, that I am the only Christian in my home and to keep the peace I decided to have this holiday elsewhere. The reason for me not spending it at my home was because not everyone likes my "friend" so therefore they weren't allowed in my home. So, in another words I wasn't going to argue. I just moved on. People will always take something good and turn it into evil so that it justifies them, and it makes them "feel" good to just hurt another individual and at what cost? I know that God sees and hears everything, even when people are against you. I wasn't going to let the enemy steal my joy especially when they didn't give the joy to me. It isn't about anything other than the celebration of the birth of Christ. I try very hard not to have confrontation with them over who they like or dislike because it has nothing to do with them. I realize you cannot change anyone, but I choose to let the Holy Spirit convict the guilty.

Chapter 6

My New Year's was quiet in 2021. I did all that I needed to do, which included a vacation to Florida to visit friends. Something I'd been trying to plan for four years. I started doing all the things that I have been putting off for a while now. I also have a new law firm handling my SSDI case now. The paperwork has been signed and delivered. Now I just keep my doctor appointments that were scheduled for my back. The disc in my lower back slipped out two days before Christmas which put me into severe pain again. It was so bad I had to take my medications again along with making a visit to my pain management doctor. See, this problem with my back is mentally stressful for me because I get to the point in which I have so much pain that I cannot stand straight or walk. Each time I am very emotional and mentally drained. I need the strength just to get out of my bed because I cannot pull myself up. I only wished that the courts would have believed me and seen I was telling the truth. I must let it all go and let my new attorney do their job. I filled out all the papers that were mailed out to me and I sent them all back including my review for my snap benefits.

It's the end of 2020, and we are heading in 2021. I was ready to say goodbye to the year and look forward to new things to happen for me. New breakthrough finally. Financial blessings flow into my life. Less fear too. So, my plan for the night is to watch the church service online.

Happy New Year 2021

Every New Year I write up a whole page of prayers and goals known as my personal resolutions. So, as I wrote that 2020 was a year with a lot of hardships and losses that I have personally had to deal with. Friends have passed from the virus and my one dear friend moved out of town. The loss of the family puppy too was difficult. My boyfriend had cancer surgery and ongoing medical issues as well. Then, finally, my case was once again denied by the appeals courts in Virginia. So, with all that has happened I have learned that my help truly had to come from the Lord, or I would not have been able to get through any of it. I do know that more now than before. I was so happy to be rid of 2020. It is forever gone and now it's a new beginning. Praise be to God.

This is my prayer for this day and the rest of the three hundred and sixty-four days moving forward. Gratitude to my God who gives me His provision and direction. For also His awesome supply of patience with me. I thank Jesus for financially seeing me through paying my bills and meeting me right where I was at. I now pray for His victory to show up with this new attorney and the firm who took on my SSDI case. I pray God will guide her and give her great wisdom in winning for me. I pray for much better health in my emotions and mental wellness. Please vanish all depression and anxiety this year so that I will no longer need to stay on medications. I ask for peace of mind too. Overall protection and health concerning my back pain. I plan to get on a better plateau with the gym and to have my cholesterol lowered. I needed to increase cardio too. Get back to taking supplements regularly as well. I've slacked a bit, but I need to get my focus back on track and I will and can do it. I want to concentrate on being less anxious and more relaxed. I plead the blood of Jesus over my emotions and my nervous system for this year. Most of all stay in His will for my life. Less stress more trust. Amen! Know that Jesus is in my boat with me, and I will not drown or go under I will get all that my heart desires including my HUD apartment in His perfect timing. Thank you, Jesus, for taking me by the hand and walking with me each day that I live.

    We have already prayed for the new year in and now we continue to trust in the Lord for everything now moving forward. I am going to get back on a diet that I have done a long time ago that did work for me. It calls for a lot of grapefruits with each meal. The gym routine will have to change also I have to do much more cardio also to burn fat faster, the past two weeks I have done only cardio to build up my immune system and keep it up there. Too much stress during the holidays so the cardio helped relieve some of it but not all of it. I deal with a lot of anxiety too. With all that is going on in the world with this virus and just trying not to get sick can be challenging. I hurt my back again the week of Christmas and I barely could move it. I had to start taking my medication for the nerves in my back. I suffer with pain that doesn't go away from the cold weather. I want to take a break from this cold weather and head to Florida but I'm not sure when that would be, I would love to go in February of this year like next month, if possible, I will have to see how this month plays out. I have two studies at the testing facility coming up. It's extremely hard to come up with money when you don't have any income for three years. So, I was able to do a back patch right before Christmas. If I can do this in my spare time it's not a problem, it helps me.

 I really cannot wait until life just gets back to normal, I mean church opens back on Fridays and the malls open later. There is nothing to do at home and I get bored so easily. Sooner or later, it will get better. I want to be able to go to the beach this summer and enjoy the summer again. I totally know what it feels like to be in a rut or stuck in a situation cause that's exactly where I have been. I'm trying to find my own way out of this but all I can do is wait. I must wait for my attorney to contact me after she receives the papers that I have filled out and mailed back to her. My heart's desire right now is that I just get my feet back on track and that I win this case and that my lawyer does her job. I want to put this all behind me and get on with my life once and for all. God make this happen for me I pray and ask you. I also want all my bills paid. Please provide for me in every step of the way. Amen! I repeat these prayers daily each day. I know that at times it sounds like I have no faith but that's not the case at all I do have faith I'm just mentally exhausted by this whole entire process and how it didn't work out with my last attorney and with the appeals court and now I just don't feel I have the fight in me to keep this going much longer. I want to focus on other things like filling out applications for my HUD apartment and hope to get one soon.

    I feel that I am not asking for something so out of reach or that it's too much to ask for, but I need to ask anyway, so Lord please hear my daily prayers and know my heart. Let this year, 2021, be my year filled with blessings from heaven. Open the windows and gates of financial prosperity. In Jesus's name I pray. I would like to include some of my daily prayers so that it will bring comfort to someone who is probably praying for the same things as I am or in a similar situation also.

To start out the year I decided to get a new haircut short, angled bob. I needed something to help me feel better about myself. So, I started taking better care of myself because over the last few years I have not been doing so well. I also started my chiropractic treatments again because the back is agitating me due to the cold weather. In other words, I seriously need to live in a warm climate. I would like to retire to Florida where the sun is out, and it doesn't get the cold that goes through your bones.

In addition, I have been recovering mail in regard to my SNAP benefits from the welfare department for my renewal. Come to find out that they keep questioning my paperwork from my current chiropractor. Once again, I had to send all the necessary documentation to the department including the cover letter from my attorney. There shouldn't be any questions to even ask but I made a call to the supervisor to report this behavior. Let me explain, every six month the welfare department follows me, like almost hounding me, for proof of why I can't work and all doctor's records which is not fine with me. The problem I have is the same people who constantly ride me are the same ones giving illegal immigrants free benefits including money to food stamp cards to those who aren't born here at all.

This is a dilemma because American people who have worked and paid taxes all their lives run into hardships and many need help. And when we try to get that help, they harass you because they gave you something. I have witnessed many times people who attend to go to Social Services show up with multiple children who they claim as their own and they at not even that person's child or children, yet they get everything as easy as blinking their eyes. No questions asked of them. They collect money for each child and hundreds of dollars in WIC and food stamps. This is a growing problem and unless you have had to depend on them for help this is the torment one will go through.

Losing a job or not being able to work anymore is devastating enough for anyone to ever endure. Certain counties may operate differently and treat people like every human being and not charity cases. It makes you feel ashamed to ask welfare for anything. But most have absolutely no choice. I thought that I should try to get on unemployment see where that would wind me up at. Wouldn't be able to get that because I'm applying for disability, and I haven't worked in four years. So, we get nothing, totally unfair. This is our government and this needs to change. There are so many things going on in this county that aren't right. But I have leaned on God to help me sort it all out and some things I will not be able to figure out. For example, why things don't go as easy as we would like them to be? Somewhere along the line there are obstacles that try every day to get in the way of God's will for us.

I think the main thing is to stay focused on the now and not be so concerned with the latter. I say to myself this too shall pass just like everything else. It's simple to know what his will is for us, if you're in the word and you're reading and your standing righteous which is right standing and you're in constant communication with Him and applying what the word says to your life that is his perfect will for your life.

Some may say that history repeats itself well I can agree that certain things may happen again and again for a reason for which we may not know why. Let's break this down into simpler terms. With my case trying to get my SSDI to get approved through the courts system and now having to hire a new attorney and going through all the same doctors, having tests upon tests just to get more medical records is something I had to do repeatedly. So yes, history does repeat itself.

Just to touch base on the current situation in my life I am back to seeing pain management and chiropractic care for my back pain. The cold weather doesn't help me at all, I suffer with arthritis in my lower lumbar every winter. I must have and had several injections also. This is mentally draining on me because it is painful to keep having shots. I am scheduled to have. Covid test the day before the procedure. The doctor also is requesting an MRI for my right knee which has been giving me some problems recently. I just must keep it moving forward with the hopes that I will soon be finished with this whole entire ordeal. Over three years is long enough for anyone to wait, but I didn't have the right attorney from the beginning, and I had to stick with them until it was time for me to move on. I had three court appearances and three appeals and still was denied so my trust is not exactly in men at this point. My new attorney seems to be more intelligent with what she is doing. I trust in God to pull me out of this mess that's pretty much it in a nutshell.

The application has been completed by my lawyer and soon I will receive the paperwork to sign and mail back to social security. In the meantime, I haven't been feeling well at all. I have been sick to my stomach and throwing up for a few days already. The tiredness is rough for anyone to deal with been in bed for four days already. I was not approved for an MRI test on my right knee because Medicaid will not pay for certain tests and X-rays which is very frustrating. When the doctor needs to treat a person and they have no idea what's going on or what they are looking at and how to treat a person and you cannot be treated because the insurance you have will not cover it makes it also difficult for someone to deal with. This gives me a great amount of stress daily. So, in the meantime I had to stay in pain because I cannot get the proper treatment. Welcome to the world of Medicaid. Where the doctors are garbage and so is the treatment that you get from this type of care. I need to explain the royal treatment of being on a low income or government program for healthcare. It had become very challenging to first find a primary care doctor who knows how to treat you without the judgement of looking at you like you're loser. Second is that when you have an appointment to see one, they must be in the network of Medicaid you may be the first one to the office, but you be sitting there for two to three hours before they see you, why? Because they don't get paid as much as they would if you had regular health care insurance. I have had many times been told by these treating physicians that they barely get paid at all from Medicaid, so they don't feel your worth the extra effort in helping you feel better. I have experienced this from primary to chiropractic and pain management doctors as well. Imagine being in pain and not feeling well at all and the physician comes into the office and says to your face "Medicare doesn't pay me much at all, but I will take you on as a patient anyway." How embarrassing is this to hear repeatedly.

As I said before, they don't cover most tests like MRI'S and medications. What does a person then think or do in my case? It's not right on all levels. I am extremely mortified by the reaction of most. I'm a patient person but there have been times I have had to switch up doctors because of this happening to me. When applying for any type of government assistance think twice because it's a roller coaster ride from the beginning.

I was literally so sick in bed for four days of vomiting and headaches that I landed in the emergency room one Friday afternoon. I had a very bad migraine with terrible pain beyond. While I was there, I had a CAT scan of my head and was giving fluids through IV, one morphine shot and one pain killer just to get rid of the nauseous and migraine pain. I suffer from migraines often and I get very sick with them so a few years ago I started going to my pain management doctor who treated me with prescriptions. Along with that I have a bad back and neck, so no one really knows how I get them but it's not good. My right knee was giving me some problems and now we are trying to get the MRI approved to find out what is going on with my knee pain. I say to God, "How much more can I deal with at the same time this is getting to be way too much for me to deal with. It isn't like it's one or two ailments but it's everything all at once?" I am sensing through the spirit that I am being physically attacked because I am headed for a serious breakthrough soon and which is something I have been praying for the past three years now plus. In my mind, there is no other reason I am going through all of this mentally and physically. Except that God is on the move for me. I can feel the fight or the pulling of good versus evil and God verses satin. Some may say I am crazy but my close friends who have known me for some time would say the same thing. God is lining me up for something great in my life. I don't know why I believe this, but I do. I can feel it with the gift I have called discernment.

The Lord gives many gifts to His children if they are open to it, and I have received this gift when I was a very young Christian. If it wasn't for the gift of discernment guiding me through my life at different times and situations, I wouldn't be here now to even tell you about it. It must be perfected like anything else you have to perfect it and practice this. You will allow you to know what spirits you always are around, maybe with people or places or even things. It comes from the Holy Spirit, not your own mind. I can be in a crowded room full of people, and I can tell what spirit or attitudes are in the room. Other times it can be used as a warning, also being in places you may not know are dangerous.

I've learned a lot but not enough in this life. I do have trouble understanding things sometimes like why good people always have it hard and the bad ones have it easy. Or at least it seems like that. My biggest question right now is how does Jesus see us in His eyes? What I mean is that there are the wealthy and the poor, so what is His will for the people who are living close to poverty is that His will for them? I want to know when the Bible states that God wants the best for "US" meaning His children who serve Him. The true "Christian" what does the word best really mean? Does He want to see us having financial stability or lack? I know that clearly the Bible states He owns all the silver and gold and a thousand cattle on a hill, but it is His will that we be lacking for nothing financially, too. Then why do we live life close to lower than he expected by not being able to support ourselves financially? I have read over and over about blessing, but I need to have a much better understanding on how Jesus views that. I was always a working person and now, I have come to a crossroad in my life that I can no longer work due to limited mobility of my back. As far as me standing seven hours a day is over for me. Also, I have other mental challenges such as anxiety. Since my mom passed away in 2012. It's been very difficult for me to wrap my head around that she is no longer here with me. I now know that she is in a much better place, and I didn't like seeing her in pain. I just had a hard time thinking it was her time to go. From there, I developed very bad anxiety and depression in which I am being treated. The holidays are not the same anymore, it's almost like it's frozen in time and you wish you could get back to that time, but you can't. I have also been dealing with the loss of my good friend from this virus which hasn't been easy because I was at her home all the time, especially at Christmas time, we would bake cookies till late in the night. Every now and again I would stop in the Catholic Church to light a candle for them both. It just makes me feel better when I do that.

Mentioning about feeling better I have not been able to work out due to the fatigue I've been dealing with. Also, I am looking forward to when I can go back and just exercise. I was scheduled for a back procedure this week which right after that I may need to rest for the next few days after that. I have had two of these injections before for the arthritis. This will give me new medical documentation for my case. I am awaiting the paperwork which needs to be signed by me and mailed back to the social security office. I have had a lot coming up all at the same time and it's very overwhelming for me, however I still must keep trusting in God because I know He is still with me in my storms. He is riding the waves with me. My physical strength is weak, but He is keeping me strong in some ways. I must admit it's difficult because I don't know the outcome, but He does. The Word says He holds my tomorrows that's all I need to know. If I have learned anything from this moving forward it's that in all ways, I cannot lean on my own understanding but to lean on His understanding in which I don't need to know all the whats, wheres, and hows at this point. I just must ride it out and know that

I won't drown. In life, you must keep fighting the good fight no matter what that leads to. We are all watching and waiting for the Lord to show up and start moving in our lives. It takes patience and perseverance to withstand what the world is going through right now. We must keep our faith up and our prayers going as we all are marching toward the mark. The mark which will lead us to our true calling and destiny.

Getting back to my previous topic of discussion on destiny, I can see that everyday we go through difficulty but one thing that I can say it that God never promised that we wouldn't go through tough times along the journey but that He would be with us through those times. He also promises that He will be with us till the end. We should be encouraged by that.

There are so many times when I questioned whether I was in the boat by myself and wondered does anyone understand what I was going through when I was pending a decision for my disability benefits. I thought that I was the only one who felt isolated in this messy situation. But when I realized that there are a lot more people probably going through almost the same thing as me. But no matter what, I still had my faith to keep me in check. I felt like I was losing my patience and I wanted to give up so many times but I couldn't because it was too far along and I was at the finish line. I said to myself, *You're almost there. Hang in there. I'm not go-*

ing to drown in this boat. I knew that Jesus was with me the whole time. The bills were coming in the mail and I was nervous about how I was going to pay them? The struggle of not having an income is extremely difficult for anyone. But that's why I had to cry out to God for financial breakthrough to come.

With the holidays approaching, now that it is November, I get the sense that I'm in for a miracle from heaven and I am strongly depending on one too. I need my SSDI to get an approval because it's now been three years of fighting. I tend to get super emotional this time of the year and if I need something to be done, I always try my hardest not to procrastinate, but I had to make all of my routine doctor appointments for the year including the eye doctors. I need to get my Medicare because being on Medicaid isn't working for me anymore. For the most part trying to find certain doctors and specialists are impossible with this limited insurance. However, I have to deal with it for now until my breakthrough comes. God is Faithful to me always has been always will be I know this delay may be a blessing in disguise. I can see that Jesus is gathering up all the money for me and is getting ready to pour out a huge blessing. The other day I was outside and I always tend to look around for the red Cardinal birds.

Last year I saw them all the time. The Cardinal bird comes around Christmas time they are a symbol of reassurance that your loved one is always with you when you need them all you need to do is look for them. So, if your loved one has passed away and they are in heaven it means that they are near and visiting you.

So, I am awaiting to see them soon. It makes me feel better to know that they are still with us even if we can't see them or talk to them anymore. Well, a least in the person-to-person state. I do know that God has His angels looking out for us and they also protect us all of the time. The Bible states that we entertain messengers of angels. Most may not know what this means so I will explain this so that you may have a better understanding. Have you ever been someplace and out of nowhere someone walks up to you knows your name and speaks to you only for a few minutes then vanishes and you never see them again but somehow you felt it was almost magical? I can give to an example of something that had happened to my boyfriend we were in a store and none was around and a gentlemen dressed in a priest's gown walked right into this store and walked right up to my boyfriend and said to him, "Hello David I feel the need to pray with you I know you're very sick."

Then I happen to walk over to him he was speaking with the gentlemen then he looked at me and gave me a medal and after that we both turned around, he was gone like into midair I even said, "Where did he go?" He was nowhere to be found even in the parking lot. So, I gather he definitely as a messenger sent by God to pray because my boyfriend was soon to be undergoing cancer surgery that week. Amazing I thought. So, sometimes, you just have to believe such things do occur and without questioning it. Just receive the blessing and move on. I may not have mentioned that I have a boyfriend now going on three years and he has had cancer in his intestines and colon area. However, the surgery went quite well. He took a while to recover but eventually he did. Right now, he has been diagnosed with lymphoma cancer in the lymph nodes but not needing treatment as of yet, so again we thank the good Lord for that. I keep telling him that, "We all are going to face God one day just not today." Count your blessing. Name them one by one because no one is guaranteed tomorrow. Live life to the fullest with each and every moment don't take anything for granted. Love the Lord with all your heart and your mind and your soul. He truly deserves the best of us.

Take time out from your busy day just to stop and say Thank-you Jesus for all you gave me and for your provision through life. My list just keeps getting bigger and bigger to give thanks there isn't enough paper to write it all down on. Really, I'm telling you the truth God is so faithful and true to His word. No one loves us more than He does. Sometimes, you may see that things don't always go according to the way we want things to go I myself have been dealing with this many times over but I do know that God does have a plan for my life and although you may not see it now but he does work behind the scenes. The delays we find ourselves in day to day are blessings in disguise and or a protection of something he knows ahead that we do not know of so he may cause a delay or keep something held back in a sense. Keep an open mind with this.

We are not working on our timeline as per say when you totally surrender something, no matter what it may be to God nod let it go it's going to be on his time table which is very different from ours here on earth. Let's put it this way, one day here is twenty-four hours but one day in the heavens can be one year because in heaven there is no "time." If that weren't true then why wouldn't Jesus know the date or time when He would return? We just know because the Bible states only the father knows the hour.

In the natural, we are all impatient at times and we want things to move at the speed of light when it comes to prayers but it doesn't work that way no prayers that are life changing or have an impact in our life is answered as soon as we ask. That is because we have to be diligent with our prayers and be continuing in prayer and communing with God always. Throughout the morning, day, and evening in constant communication to the Father in heaven. This is what relationship is.

Still God's love for us is unconditional and He wants to commune with us daily. I'm not saying you have to spend hours upon hours quoting scriptures and memorizing all the chapters in the Bible but even if you sing a song in worship in your house or car you when you're listening to your iPod or streamed music as long as you know that he is just waiting for you to acknowledge that He is there wanting to hear from us.

With the time of the year when the holidays are approaching and the changes start like all the leaves fall to the ground then the weather getting a little colder at night soon we will be in the Christmas season. The lights, the trees, and decorations are so beautiful. It brings such a warm feeling inside of me. It's one of my favorite times of the year, however at the same time it is the most emotional time too. It can bring you to happy tears or sad tears because of those who went home to "glory." But the happy ones I believe that they are reminders of "hope." Christmas isn't about a guy in a red suit or reindeer or even presents its really about God giving us the gift, of His only Son Jesus to earth for us so they we may have salvation through Jesus- Yeshua the Messiah. The tree is a symbolic for Jesus being the tree of life (just like His cross made of a tree), and the lights on the tree are the lights of God. The branches of the tree are his arms stretched out for the world. So, it does go a whole lot deeper than the tale we all believed as children but it's important to know the truth and the real meaning behind Christmas. To further state the fact that it also means Christ's Mass so we celebrate in that the birth of the Son Jesus. Even though he wasn't born in the month of December Everyone has the right to choose what they want to believe and I will not argue over a religion or a concept I will just tell you what I've been brought up and raised up with believing. I think that being we all have a choice to believe or not to it's pretty simple.

Let's just say we all agree that we have choices in this life and some of those choices that we have made or make are in our control. For example, we can control our thoughts and even how we would react to it. What we cannot control is the outcome of an action due to that choice. So, always think before making a life altering choices because no one is guaranteed tomorrow. We are now all going through a World crisis with the Covid-19 virus that came in March of 2020, and we are now at the second wave of it worse than before news media reports three thousand people a day are getting infected daily. Hospitals are reaching higher than normal admissions of people infected and being tested positive. Right now, there are discussions of another state lockdown, in which we as the state of New Jersey cannot afford to have that happen again. Small businesses will shut down for good while others continue to lose money. Retail stores have been going out of business for the past few months now and it's only getting worse. The job market is closing in and there isn't much to find now especially in retail or even being a cashier. I was a cashier and I really enjoyed it very much. As for me now I can no longer even if I wanted to go back I can't due to the fact that I cannot stand up too long without severe back and leg pain. Those days are long gone for me.

So much more is going on in the world this was the election year for Donald Trump and Joe Biden. I actually voted for the first time ever. The outcome has yet to be resolved on who has won to be "President "of the United States. Due to votes being tossed and not counted correctly and all the other things that illegally happened. We now may have to wait until January to see the real result. We do pray for this nation for God's intercession on this dishonesty and put the right person in the White House to do the job. We also need to continue to pray for God to heal us land from this deadly virus. There is a lot at stake now and Everyone is feeling the tension of all of this. I know for myself that I am very stressed over a lot of what's happening in my own life and all this outside my door things make it only worse. We all are kind of in fear of being infected by someone who is sick but we cannot live our life that way either. I personally will not live my life afraid every minute of every day thinking about such negativity.

The word clearly states that God doesn't give us a spirit of fear he gives us power and a sound mind. No matter what we are to remain calm and at peace in knowing that "fear" is not of God. Did you know that when you worry and fear your questioning your own faith? It actually puts doubt in your faith. That's why I'm still going to trust in my God and Savior all of the time. No matter what the situation looks like on the surface or outside its what matters in the spirit realm.

In the unseen spirit realm is the key to all powerful belief and strong faith. Believing in the unseen. Faith is the substance of things hoped for, the evidence of things not seen. (Hebrews 11:1). Getting ready for Thanksgiving just around the corner everyone is rushing around getting all the foods that need to be cooked etc. Making lists of the dinner and deserts. In the hustle and bustle of the holiday season people tends to get moodier and nastier. The parking lots get crazy and everyone wants to get in and out of the stores as soon as possible, even if that means cutting you off to get that spot or pushing you in the line or even cutting lines. Question is "Why?" "Why does everyone seem to have no patience when it comes to the holidays?" Is it because we are so geared driven by the speed and the mentality of hurry up that we literally miss what the true meaning of it really means?

Thanksgiving Day is a day when we truly should sit down and Thank God for all he has already given to us and what he brought us through. We would be nothing and have nothing if it wasn't for Him. Everything that we have is all because He gave it to us just like He gave His only begotten Son as a gift to us for the redemption of sin. So even when we mess up God still keeps on giving to us. Reason we serve a Good God.

When things don't go the way, we planned what do we do? Well, I will tell you what we should do. We should remain in the Spirit and in His presence at all times don't drift away with your own thoughts. We have to seek His face daily and pray constantly for God's provision in any circumstance. Think about this, if your walk is right, you're in the will of God. If you have a false sense of security about something in your walk and something doesn't quite feel right to your chances are that you may need to search your heart and get it right before him. This doesn't mean that your plan isn't good it may be its just not the right timing, or its being delayed for some other reason in which you don't know. But whatever the delay is and for how long Trust in God no matter what. He is working on your behalf behind the scenes. You don't need to know all about the who, what, where, or when's, you just have to believe that whatever it is will work out for you, and it will be also for the Glory of God. So, overall that testimony that you will later speak about after that prayer gets answered will be so that everyone would know that it was God who caused it to happen to you.

For the most part some things in life just had to happen and not everything that happens bad to a person is the devil doing it. Sometimes, God will put a roadblock in your way as a means of distraction or to get your attention off of the thing that happened and onto him. Just like when Peter was on the water Jesus called to him to walk toward him and because for a second Peter took his eye off of Jesus and looked down on the water and he almost drowned. Another reason something had to happen is so that God can take you from your current location and move you into your destiny. No matter what the purpose of the situation is always be aware of the "delay."

Another example of God causing a delay is not answering your prayer right away. In his word it speaks of the words He uses which are "yes" or "wait." But the delay may seem so long for the most part but He does have a reason for it we just have to trust in that. He may be preventing you for something of disaster or preparing you in advance for something better. So be patient when you see a delay in a prayer.

The fact that the Bible states, "If God before me who can be against me?" I like to think of it this way, He is working it all out for my good. In everything you do always remember this one thing. "The Cross before me the World behind me." Keep your focus on the cross because that is where hope is found. The world cannot give you Jesus and the world can't take Him away from you. The world cannot give you peace, love or even joy also and certainly not everlasting life. The world can't take it away.

When I think of all the Names of Jesus, I'm amazed because he is all of them at different times in your life, as well as mine. Here are just a few of the names:

> Yeshua- Jesus, Messiah, Jehovah, El Elyon (The most high God) Adonai (Lord Master), Yahweh (Lord Jehovah), Jehovah Nissi (The Lord my banner), Jehovah Raah (The Lord that heals), Jehovah Shaman (The Lord is there), Jehovah Tsidkenu (The Lord of our righteousness), Jehovah Mekoddishkem (The Lord who sanctifies you), El Olam (The everlasting God), Elohim (God), Qanna (Jealous), Jehovah Jireh (The Lord will provide), Jehovah Shalom (The Lord is peace), Jehovah Shaboath (The Lord of hosts).

There are over three hundred and sixty-five names of God used here is another list of what God is to me:

> Jesus, Alpha and Omega, (The beginning and the End), Immanuel, (God with Us), King of Kings, (Above all Gods), Light of the World

(Brings light into darkness), Morning Star, Prince of Peace, (Not as the World gives), Wonderful counselor (He will give you counsel), Lamb of God (As the lamb sacrificed), Savior of the World, (Redeemer), The Good Shepherd, (The one who attends to all his sheep), The Way, (Straight), Lord of Lords, Anointed One, Bread of Life, (Food for your soul), Chief Cornerstone (The Rock), Great High Priest, Holy and Righteous One (Pure), Lord of Glory, Messiah, (The one True God), Teacher, The Truth, and Word of God.

Chapter 7

My true heart's desire is to get back into the music ministry and for God to use me in the church that I am attending now. Since I was thirteen years old, I sang in choirs within the church congregation in every church that I attended. When I was attending a non-denominational church youth group, I was also in the music ministry serving God on Friday night services.

I know this is my calling and I am getting ready for an open door. I have been praying for some time for Jesus to place me where He wants to use me. Constant and continuing to seek His face regarding this even in the pandemic of the world as we are currently still in. I will do as I am instructed to do when the Holy Spirit guides me to the door that will open before me, and the right opportunity will present itself to me. This I know. We always hear a lot about finding your "CALLING," this means whatever you know in your heart to so for God you find what that thing is, and you go before Him and do it. That given talent you have, you should use it for the purposes of GOD. There is no better feeling than knowing and being used to minister to anyone who will listen. Mine is in song. I truly hope that you all find your true calling and the rewards are great. If you aren't sure what is maybe trying to think of that thing that you're good at and stay within that field. It may branch out from that field, but this takes some time to figure out with God and through your prayer life. Ask Him to show you what yours is...

Even though we may be in a global pandemic that doesn't mean that we should stop all the things that we have done before like praying. If you have a church and it is open then that is your opportunity to go in a be in the presence of God no matter what. I have on multiple made a point to continue to go I attended weekly Bible study and each time I had a chance before I have also donated food and stopped in and prayed for about 1 hour even before it got bad. I also went to the Catholic Church just to pray or light a candle for my loved ones who have gone to heaven. I pray for protection very important and healing. We cannot take this virus too lightly because it's going to affect everyone around you. At this present time Covid-19 has hit my home starting with my brother so I had to pack my suitcase and quarantined outside my home for the next ten days. As I have been exposed to the virus, I had to cancel having my back procedure since I won't be allowed into the doctor's office anyway. Guess it was an intervention for me not to have anything done at this time.

Remember in the beginning when I spoke about timing and delays? This is a delay of some sort, but I cannot let this control what I think. At this point, it's not about what we all think it's about the reality that this is the new now and the old way that we are all used to is long gone and the way that we used to do things are different on all levels. At the gym the locker rooms are closed off and the lockers are limited use only because they have zipped tied most of the lockers. The showers are totally closed. Although wearing a mask and cleaning each machine is mandatory now and yet there will be people who will not wipe the machine down regardless of a virus or not. Everyone's life was altered by this pandemic at some point or other. It made an impact on my life, which made me more anxious and depressed due to being isolated ten days at a time and not being able to feel safe anymore, so I left that for my therapist to determine why she is still treating me. In life you need someone to talk to you and help you cope with life's ups and downs. It makes me feel better just to know that I can talk with someone, even if they don't have any answers for me. On a good note, my church will soon be opening for services on Sunday. I have been praying to be used by God for months and months and to get involved in a music ministry. Soon after praying for about two years my church is asking for help in all areas of the ministry and looking for people who want to be a part and get involved, I have put in my request to get involved and that I can sing again. So, this may be my opportunity to fulfill my "calling" after all these years. I would want nothing more than to get back into being a blessing and minster for God. I know that I am going through a whole bunch of trials and tribulations and although they are very overwhelming for me I won't "let go" of God's promises for me. I stand on one very important scripture, and it is (Jeremiah 29:1) Where He has a plan for me and a plan to help me and not hurt me and a promising future and hope. Another scripture is Psalms (91:1-16). We dwell under the shadow of the Highest Almighty. Which means under the protection of God we shall dwell. This also states that no destruction will come to us nor shall any plague come near our dwelling. This is giving me so much hope that we have this promise from God. I truly believe this was his covenant with us.

Getting back to a time where I can just remember when I was working seems like so long ago even though it's been four years later, I felt more complete sometimes. I feel like what happened to me that I had to just stop working when I did because for me it was like a dead stop with no going back. One day, I was able to deal with back pain and now I cannot even think of standing on my feet for more than an hour. So, when I originally applied for my disability, I never would have thought that it takes so much out of a person mentally let alone physically. I have been so tired and literally exhausted to the point where I can sleep for days on end. The time it's taking to process and then to have to appeal and keep appealing then having to start all over again to filling out a whole new application is way too exhausting. I don't have it in me to keep fighting this, so I have absolutely no choice because it's totally in my new attorney's hands. I am hoping and praying that this part of my life will soon be all over and I can get ahead of my life with that promised future that God so promised me.

For anyone who is going to go through the thought of applying for SSDI let me be the first one to tell you- put your seatbelt on because you're in for the ride of your life. The timing of the process means that you must be out of work for one year and being treated for the same amount of time or more just to apply then after that it takes another year for a court date. So, it does take two to five years on average for most people. The other thing I can say is that you will need is a good support system and good family members to be behind you along with the right doctors to back you up. Christian people in your corner are the best because they will pray you through it and not get tired of you asking for prayer. I have prayed with my friends and my church has been very understanding. They also prayed for me multiple times as well. I also have a prayer chain going with unity for extra prayers. They send me all kinds of books, pamphlets, and letters for prayer requests. I am so thankful for my resources behind me who show me they care. When this is all said and done, I will do as I am instructed to do by the Holy Spirit as I'm led to do. I know in my heart there is a reason aside from all this and a lesson to be learned only right now I don't know what that is at this point. I was asleep one morning when I received a call from social security but they didn't leave a message, so I decided to call them back. They said that they may want to go over my work history, so I must call them back on Tuesday. I also contacted my attorney, and she told me that they may not have received my application yet. The mail has been backed up for months now, so I will have to wait until they get my signed application. While on the phone I asked a few questions to them like how long does this process really take? I was told that it should take a few months because what they do is read the application then get the medical records and it goes before a panel and they go over it and make a decision if they don't give it to you then and it's denied you can appeal it which I already did four times. Overall, it takes a few months.

Shortly after my birthday, I was driving home from Fairfield and a huge piece of ice flew from across the highway on the complete opposite side from where I was driving in the middle lane hit my brand-new car.

All I can see is this ice coming at me ninety miles an hour and boom right on my hood then the windshield and over the roof of the car I was stunned. I just kept on driving. The next day, we still had ice and salt all over the place due to the twenty inches of snow we had the. I got it before I brought the car to the Auto body shop to get the estimate and while looking the car over, we noticed more damage like scratches and chips on the windshield. Then I called my insurance company to make a claim and they sent the adjuster out to see the car. So now I will be receiving a check for half the amount of the estimates and that leaves me having to most likely pay the deductible. I'm not going to do anything yet until I can have that deductible eaten up. The Auto body shop said that they will work with me. Trust in God to work it out for me, right? Yes, I have to. What else can I do? I don't have the money to even come close to paying for car repairs now. It just puts me between a rock and a hard place because the car is leased. With a lease it must be in perfect condition upon returning it to the dealership at the end of the lease term. I'm very thankful that I always have a new car. However, it's an expense either way but I'm looking forward to the day when I won't have to make car payments and own my car. I also would love to have my own apartment through the HUD low-income housing authority system. I keep trying to fill out applications to see if I can win the lottery for the apartments so most of them have a two-year waiting list.

I will now have a lot more things to tell my therapist in my next session. The conversation always starts out like this, "How are you feeling today? My reply, "Well, I'm not doing too good at coping with all that I am dealing with between my health issues with my back and just not feeling good mentally. Then on top of all that my head is going a mile a minute." See my pain management doctor wanted to have me get an MRI to treat me for a knee problem I've been having for a few months. On another note, my insurance company has denied the test without the authorization department finalizing a decision, so my doctor had to appeal that decision on my behalf. In the meantime, I must find a simpler way to treat my pain in the leg which I have been wrapping up and just putting heat on it for now. I also have been praying over it daily for healing. It's just strange that the knee starts hurting while I'm sleeping, and it wakes me up in the middle of the night.

I had called my insurance company to find out a few things such as when or could I have the test. They inform me that the doctor's office hasn't even tried to send the documentation to the authorization department yet. So where do I go from now dealing with office staff who simply won't do their jobs. On another note, I did finish up with the chiropractor who I was going to for the past year and now I'm going to take a break for about two months now and will go see a new one in the same town because I didn't feel a difference with the prior treatment plan in which he was giving me, time to move forward. Talking about moving forward SSA has received all of my files and is starting the process now and has been assigned to an employee of SSA to read through it. Prayers are important now more than ever so that we all move forward and get ready to make it to the finish line once and for all. Praise be to God when this is finished it will be a testimonial for everyone to hear.

My car was damaged with a sheet of ice that flew across the highway and hit the hood then bounced to the roof and slid off the back of the car, so I need to get this fixed. All estimates are still being taken care of. Had to make another phone call to my car insurance company about resending the adjuster out again for more scratches that were found after the fact. But I'm sure it will all work out.

I finally had the opportunity to speak with my best friend about making a visit for a few days to hang out and just catch up so within the next upcoming weeks or so I will be going down toward the shore area to her house. It's been so long since she moved out of this area. It will be good to see her again. We are planning to go on another cruise possibly in 2022 or 2023 if all goes well. On the last cruise ship that we went on in 2017, was called "THE ANTHEM OF THE SEAS." It was a huge ship and we had so much fun and to this day we still talk and laugh about the good times that we had. That was where I came up with the idea to write a book as I was in Haiti on a bench having lunch that the crew had cooked for all of us who took that excursion. When we stood in line for our food, we found a seat on the benches table when I turned to her and made a comment about writing a book about my life. As we laughed and giggled all throughout the day. I am now searching for upcoming cruises. But as of right now they are being delayed because we are still in the pandemic.

    I have been in contact with my attorney with regards to my application and it finally was received by the SSA, and it is waiting to be appointed to the person to have my file. My attorney informed me that we are not at the hearing level yet. I have gone as far as changing the primary doctor and getting all my medical records sent to one doctor. I also am heading over to see a neurologist in the next week because the migraines that I have been having are getting much worse and I have pains in my head all the time. I have been having to take my migraine medication much more frequently than normal. I was in the emergency room in January 2021 for the migraine which caused me to be very sick for days. While I was there, I had several tests including a CAT scan of my head. Then I was sent home a few hours later with more medication including pain pills. I'm not sure what I will do. My pain management doctor who was treating me left the Riverside medical group, so I either will stay with the new one that took his place or find someone completely new. These are the things I spoke to my attorney about in our last conversation. To be continued, but I did receive a letter in the mail from SSA that they are now going to forward any communications to my represented attorney instead of contacting me from now on. I say to myself good idea because I rather not have to get involved with this if I don't have too.

Moving forward, I started filling out applications for low-income housing with the hopes of getting my very own apartment when this is all finished. I'm standing on God's promise (Philippians 4:8) which says, "Finally brethren whatever things are true, whatever things are noble, whatever things are just, whatever things are pure, whatever things are lovely, whatever things are good report if there be any virtue and there is anything praiseworthy meditate on these things." So, I will do this as well. I am thinking of a new beginning and a better life for myself and my sanity. I'm a huge believer in dreaming big when I do dream so I will do that too. The next step is to be determined and must just sit back and wait till the next thing comes. A week later, I received my lottery number for a place in Hazlet, NJ soon so things are starting to look up for me.

Things will get back to somewhat normal again soon is what I keep telling myself going along with my therapy sessions every three weeks does help with the things that you want to talk about with someone else's ears on the situations. One of my sessions was to talk about how I am feeling emotionally. Unfortunately, I had to tell the truth I said that on the outside I appear to be fine. I mean I don't like complaining about the aches and pains I have daily- including more severe migraines than before and things of that nature. If it's not one thing it's another. So, instead I said, "I'm very frustrated in so many ways mentally waiting this long with this unbearable process from the filling out the application for my SSDI to the denial and then all the appeals and now having to have a new attorney and now having to start over and wait and again wait. It's so stressing me out that I feel it's stripping away my dignity because I must be so dependent on everyone around me for support. Just the mental anguish of not having a salary at all is way too much for anyone to even comprehend. The past four years I have been more than obedient and have done everything I was asked to do, and I seriously need this breakthrough like never before. This time around I am getting my ducks in a row one by one with new records and doctors."

I'm now being seen by a neurologist for the migraines that I have been battling for years. The doctor is going to try to send me for an MRI if she can get it approved with Medicaid. I informed her that my pain management doctor tried but couldn't get it approved. Besides that, he quit the group he was in, which leaves me without one, so I must find a new pain management doctor for my back issues. I also will be giving the chiropractic treatment a rest for a couple of months. I think that all the manipulation to the spine may be aggravating the muscles and discs even more, so they need a rest. The question that my therapist has asked me, "How do you persevere with all this going on in your life?" My reply was honestly, "I've been praying a lot and attending my church each week. I want to get into the music ministry too." She said, "It's good for you to use meditation especially if it helps with anxiety." Until the next session three weeks from now.

Chapter 8

Springtime is here today was about sixty degrees out and I walked around the flea market and bought myself something I could use. I bought my very first travel kit. It included a passport holder, luggage tag and a wallet for all boarding passes and other documents. They came in a box with all three things for three bucks. Putting into action my thoughts of my travels and said to myself, *wow this is awesome buy it now*. And this will be the best gift for me. It made my day even though I wasn't feeling good at all. I had another migraine last night into the next day. I do hope we can find out why I feel this way all the time.

Besides that, tomorrow is the first reopening of church Passover Sunday, and I am going to go. I'm excited to be going back into the house of God. Spring means new things and new beginnings just as flowers bud as we look forward to the harvest. I look for God to do new things in my life and breakthrough. We are entering into the most Holy time of the year. This is the time for the Christian to be reunited together as a body of Christ in worship and in truth. I praise God for what

He brought me out of a bad winter. A dark place in the wilderness and His protection from me getting this virus that's still infecting people all over the place. Once again, I made it through. But only by His Grace and Mercy which is new each morning. Sometimes, I fail to see that during the storm because I'm right smack in the middle of it but each time the storm seems to let up, I do feel and start to see some light shining through the clouds. I'm also waiting for the storm clouds to pass, and the rainbow once again will be before my eyes.

One week later, let's begin by saying I've had more doctor appointments these past few weeks than I can even keep up with. Starting with neurology for the migraines I've been dealing with for more than a year they go back to my early thirties and now I just can't ignore them anymore, so my doctor is wanting me to get an MRI along with the medications in a spray. Then after a few days they called me back and wanted to see me in the office again on Friday of the same week two of the other doctors requested to see me. I also made an appointment with the pain management. The only thing is there was no doctor there, only a nurse practitioner. This is how this conversation took place. As I was sitting there for almost an hour waiting for someone, I said a quick prayer. "God, I come to you now asking you for the words to say and for help with getting these people on point with me for my disability." So, when she came in,

I spoke to her short and sweetly but got my point across once and for all. I let them know I've been treated many times, done shots and physical therapy also chiropractic and I have been dealing with chronic pain since I was seventeen years old when I juried my back working. I applied for temporary disability then after it ran out, I hired an attorney for permanent disability. After being denied several times and things not working out with the attorney in which I had for three years I had to find a new attorney who in fact filed a new application for me. I need now to have my medicines updated and my record as soon as possible along with a letter for SSDI basically saying I cannot work anymore, period. I'm not playing games with injections or surgery I just want a letter and their support. They said it is not a problem they will indeed help me with whatever I need. Now that they are onboard with me when I need my medical records sent out to my primary doctor.

I just really need some favor, God. Something must start going my way here. I am so tired of fighting for this I'm running out of energy. My nerves are on edge. Please take the load off my back and let this go in my favor with the courts and with my lawyer now. I need breakthrough. I need for the person who is handling my file at social security to be touched from God and have a heart to see the proof in front of him or her. I don't want to have to go to their doctors or court for that matter let this be approved for me quickly and effectively immediately in Jesus's name I pray...

These are just some of the emotions I feel daily. Although I do talk about this in therapy, I talk to Jesus every morning, noon, and night. I know He understands the constant amount of stress I am under each month that goes by then turn that into years of waiting. I have no choice to wait on God to make a move on my behalf. This is the end of it. I'm going to cross over the finish line and win this if it's the last thing I get to do in this lifetime of fighting for something that will shape my entire rest of my life. This is my income and my health including better healthcare insurance and a future. With the hopes of winning an apartment through HUD low-income housing. I have filled out several applications and been on many waiting lists. So, it's up to Jesus to fulfill His promises to me. I have done all I can do in my strength I cannot do anymore; this is where I ride this out. Just like the storm in life this is my storm and the waves knocked me down more than once but I'm back on my feet to win and I won't settle for less than.

On another note, I am waiting and expecting to hear back from my church about me getting involved in the music ministry, I haven't heard anything yet. I'm still going before the Lord with this too. I know in His time He will open the door for me to sing. I want to be used by God for Him this is my desire to sing and to fulfill my calling also. It was a few weeks later when church opened, I spoke to the head of the music ministry about me getting involved and I was informed of how the process works at the church. First, I would have to become a member. Then they would have me come in and sing for them so that they can hear me sing then they let me know. It may take some time, but I will do whatever I need to do because this is something I really want for my life.

As we proceed with all my doctor's appointments now seeing a neurologist and pain management. I just had my MRI for my lower lumbar back. Next will be in two weeks for the head, they want to find out why I'm getting so many migraines and headaches. I am to follow up and make sure all these test results get forwarded to the doctor's offices so I can get treated.

Going to my church all through the Easter holidays got me through a lot of this and gave me hope that it will all work out in the end. The service was very good and encouraging. Pastor preached one of the services (Jeremiah 29:11). That God has a plan for my life. I know He has a plan for my life. My case is moving forward in the right direction. I just mailed out another set of forms to the SSA. The forms were daily function sheets with about five pages of questions to be filled out by a friend or family member so when I was finished with them, I made copies for myself. My attorney said she will fill out the other ones on my behalf. I am taking all the necessary actions I need to take to get this all done, and I have done just that so that there is no room for mistakes. My neurologist and pain management doctor are onboard helping me get to where I need to be with getting me my SSDI. Finally, I'm getting some sort of help but it's still very hard for me to accept that this is where my life went. At some point, I must adjust that this is the way it is for now and hope that this is all done for the glory of God's purposes. How else would He advances me financially and provide for me to the point that I will be able to support myself and my future with the cost of living? That's where "trust" comes into play. When you have no other way, Jesus makes a way in the wilderness and dark places He sends light.

If I have learned anything from this process it is that I need to rely only on Him who is the author and finisher of my faith and that He truly is my soul provider and my healer above all the medical doctors he is the only "One True God. "I cannot find the words to even begin to explain all that he has made possible for me. For me this whole thing started in July 2017, and I have been through the ringer with the disappointment of not getting my SSDI sooner or that my attorney at the time argued with the judge on the day we went to court which wasn't a good thing to do because that judge denied me after all that. Nothing seemed to make a difference on what medical records had to say, he just wasn't hearing it. It was a done deal from then on. We even appealed it three times and still denied. So, I ask myself, "Was this all Gods will that it had to happen like it did?" I guess I will never know why he caused a major delay for years, but I did learn to be more patient when waiting for God's purposes to come to pass.

I can honestly say that I have had to take a back seat and allow Him to work this all out in His time and His space. I had to let go, plain and simple. I had a very hard time doing that and no one could have told me differently to just chill out and let it go I had to learn on my own the hard way. We all live life in the fast lane quick to move and we all want things to happen at a certain speed of life but unfortunately when you're living for God it doesn't happen like that. He opens the floodgates and windows of heaven when He is ready to. The thing is this, I don't want to move ahead of him because I tend to mess things up every time, I do that. While I wait, I will continue to worship and be obedient. I will be bold and confident while I wait.

In the meantime, I entered springtime and said goodbye to the cold dead of winter. Here it is April and it's been rainy and not so warm outside. I have been attending my church services all through Easter time. I attended Sunday services as well as Friday evenings. It feels great to be back, too. I asked about becoming involved in the music ministry and was informed that I must become a member first, so I will do that soon. I know that in becoming a member tithing is an essential part of it and now I don't have any income to support that but when I do have my monthly income, I will then tithe. I've always given even when I didn't have money to give so I would give a few dollars or whatever I had on me at the time. God knows my heart is in the right place. I appreciate my church for understanding my current situation and they accept me anyway. When this is all over and done, I will as promise to give a gift to my pastor or praying over me urging my hard time. It is the least I can do.

Things are moving in a slow but steady motion with my case. My medical records are being submitted now and I am attending all my doctor's appointments. I've had all the MRIs that were requested for me to get along with pain management and neurology. My follow up appointment will be next week, and I will get a letter to add to my records. So, I ask myself, "How am I feeling overall?" Well, needless to say, we still are in a pandemic with this virus. I am gathering all my paperwork so that I can get my passport soon. This has been something that I really want to get so that when I do go back to traveling it will be easier than carrying my original birth certificate with me from place to place. The cruise lines have been cancelled and they still are not cruising until

2023. Hopefully, then I will get to go again. This can be very frustrating not being able to go anywhere. One day everything will go back to normal. I may have to get vaccinated to go on a plane too which I am not too thrilled about because I'm not one who likes getting any types of shots. But only if I must get one to ever fly. I will then because I am going to get onboard a ship and a plane at some point.

I am feeling kind of tired of waiting its feels like I have been in this stand still forever. It's like a neverending tunnel with no light at the end of it. I know this sounds like I'm in a dark place, but I am not just been very overwhelmed with anxiety because this is taking so long. I need a vacation real soon just to relax my mind. I am still in therapy, but I don't feel that therapy is making a difference, it just gives me someone to talk to. What does help me is that I still go to the gym and do more cardio now to relieve the stress. In fact, it does make a difference to work out because it gets my endorphins up and lowers my cortisol levels in my body. I have been working out since I was seventeen years old, and I will always continue to do so for the rest of my life. The only thing that I need to do now is to follow up with my doctor's reports.

I am scheduled for another stress test from my cardiologist. Each year I've had to get all checked out. Doing my part in my overall health. Last year, I was told that I do have high cholesterol and it's been hard for me to get those numbers down but I'm going to really try harder to do that this year from now on. I want to get into better shape also because I have been taking anti-depressant medication it has caused me to gain some weight. This has been bothersome for me. I was always weight conscientious and now it's a bit too much for me, however I will work on that, too. I go to the gym regularly and have been doing more cardio training as well as light stretching and resistance training. I can no longer push the weights around like I used to due to the severity of pain in my lower back.

That has been acting up bad for the past few years. I am in the process of getting to my neurologist monthly for shots as part of my treatment for my headaches which more than likely are coming from my neck and back no doubt. Getting older now has been taking a huge toll on me mentally because I'm in so much pain. I pray each day for healing. I always look to Jesus as my healer and my deliverer. I stopped at the connection desk at my church and requested a membership packet. I have listened to all the CD's that were included so now I just have to have a pastor or leader from another church that I attended to sign it for a referral so that my church can give them a call-in regard to knowing me. I did in fact reach out just recently to a pastor who knows me, and I'll be forwarding the letter to be signed. The reason for all of this is that once I can become a member of the church, I can try to get into the music ministry which I am called to do. I always knew that's one area that God has given me a very strong desire and calling for. I have been praying for this for a long time now, I just need the right doors to open for me. I know that they will, and I will see the victory in my life. I do believe that God is leading me into my destiny. I would like to share something that just recently happened to me while I was online on a social media website one day and it said this, "Click here to receive your prophetic word from God." So, I clicked onto the box and I was led to a special prayer by a pastor. He took my name and email then emailed me the very next day. This is what he said to me.

"He informed me not to let the enemy have any part in my life as far as stress and being overwhelmed. Also, that I have patience and to take one step at a time, take care of my health in the upcoming months. God is moving me in a direction that will lead me into what I am called for in Him, that I have many gifts and talents that the Lord has put inside of me, and I will be used of God. I am not to let the enemy distract me in any way from going forward."

It was amazing because everything he said was true to the exact thing that I have been feeling and going through. As the spirit moved, he continued to say a lot more about my writing and special gifts that the Lord has instilled in me. I can't say how good it is to hear a word like this from someone who prayed, and the Lord gave this word for me. Every word was to the point and couldn't be more precise, it was unbelievable. Every day I say a prayer that Jesus would talk to me and give me a word of encouragement, because I really need to be encouraged at times when the storms of life get to overwhelming for me to bear. I always ask Jesus to lift it all from me and He does. As I delight myself in the spirit of true worship, I start to feel better. My anxiety and depression start to lift, even when I wake up at 11:00 in the morning. Sometimes I don't want to get out of bed, but I push myself to go to the gym just to feel better about myself. It helps, it really does. Now that summer is on the way I will get up earlier in the mornings so I can get a head start with the gym routine and go in my pool. I do want the life of travel so I should get this vaccine but I'm still very unsure at the same time. I will see how springtime plays out with all the other tests I must have in the upcoming months. Most of all, I'm doing all that I can do for myself as far as taking control of the things I can take control over. Let God take care of the rest. I have been a little calmer knowing I have a very good attorney this time around.

I was watching TBN one morning and I heard a pastor preaching about the man at the pool and he said something that made so much more sense to me now than before he was talking about when Jesus said, "take up your mat and walk." The man was instantly healed and not because he was trying to get up that he was healed it was that he trusted Jesus that he was healed so it was a trust issue he was having. See Jesus didn't want to hear he was trying to get up he wanted the man to trust Him enough to get up. For me it was a trust issue, but I learned from this whole experience that I had to trust in the Lord fully and completely.

Chapter 9

Springtime is a time of a new season. The more rain we have the more flowers we see and the greener the grass gets. The cherry blossoms are pink and white but only last a few weeks. Then before you know it summer comes along with the heat. I like the summertime because there is more to do outdoors than being inside. I have tried to make the best of it the past four years and each year that goes by is a time for maturity. I have been very stressed and overwhelmed with the pandemic that we have been in, wearing a mask has been extremely difficult for someone who is going through menopause and had constant hot flashes. It makes me anxious to have my mouth covered while sweating from the back of my neck and from the top of my forehead and down. It takes about three minutes for it to pass. I am taking supplements called black cohosh to control the symptoms. Along with anti-depressants as well. I realized that menopause is all part of life but it's bad. I will not go for hormone therapy because it's just not well. I have been told by several doctors that it can cause ovarian cancer so I'm not even considering that. Hopefully this will go away soon. Each day I do say a quick prayer that God will lift the flashes. I've been praying more also and reading my Bible too; I find it relaxes me when I read. Exercise and working out are a huge part of keeping a healthy mind as well. If I cannot get to the gym, I exercise at home. I have the abs coaster and dumbbells. I just recently received a mini stepper. However, I don't lift weights as heavy as I used to but I do use light weights and dumbbells.

Now getting back to the real issues, things are not good in the world so I have decided to get on with my life as health conscious as I can, so I did get vaccinated with the Pfizer dose. Three weeks later is my second shot. The only thing I felt was a sore arm for a few days but unlike back pain or migraines I usually have nothing in comparison to it. I will move forward in getting my passport for this summer, next are the pictures I need. After that is completed, I will attach my vaccination card with the application if need to be. I don't want to take any chances to get sick from a stranger when I go on vacation.

I thank God for His mercies that I didn't get Covid-19 and that I have stayed healthy so far. Taking vitamins like multi and probiotics are key to starting a supplement nutrition plan. I can't express how important nutrition plays a huge part in overall wellness it's not about "diet" it's about a change in lifestyle. Consuming the right number of proteins and low on carbohydrates along with plenty of greens and fruits. I personally like blueberries and raspberries. I go for the antioxidant in each of these. Stay light on the caffeine and go for more green tea. Drinking plenty of water throughout the day to stay hydrated is very important as well. I know a lot of people nowadays really don't care about overall health or total fitness but trust me, going to a doctor to get checked out, especially for cardiology, is vital. I will be going for my second stress test in the upcoming weeks more likely next week. A full set of blood work is also an order. I don't want to find out anything when it's too late. So, take heart when I say it's in your best interest that you follow my lead. If I can help someone and make an impact on one person then I know I have done my job. In fact, that would make me smile and be happy. I care for people this is why I am giving this advice to you.

I may look good on the outside because that is what I proceed to show the outward appearance means a lot to me however that doesn't mean that inside my body hurts from pains in my lower back and having migraines all the time. It's been this way for a very long time, it's something I'm battling with every single day. I want to wake up one day without feeling this pain that runs down into my leg into my feet. It's more on the left side where that disc is herniated. If it was up to me, I wish I could have a set of new discs. I will be seeing my neurologist for injections soon. I did chiropractic also for months but no relief from that. I must find a chiropractor who does all muscle stimulation, massage therapy and the right adjustments in which I have had a hard time finding one that has it all to treat me. Again, having Medicaid makes it very difficult to have good health care. It's free so you can't expect perfection when it's free health care.

I do believe that I started having issues with my back when I was a lot younger than I had previously stated. Let me take you back to a time when I was just a little girl as far as I can remember, maybe about seven years old. When my dad left us, my brother and I had moved into my grandmother's house which was at the top of a hill on a small street. It was a thirteen-room house with four bedrooms, three bathrooms, basement fully furnished which also had a bar and a kitchen as well. In the backyard there was a huge built-in pool with a picnic table and grill. Ever since then I can still recall my grandmother who was a diabetic, had seven children and fourteen grandchildren, so this was a very big family. My mom, being the oldest child, was informed that she would become the caretaker of her mom soon after my grandmom suffered a stroke and became paralyzed which put her in a wheelchair for the rest of her life. She also had physical therapy for years in Kessler, but it didn't seem to work, her right side was not going to ever improve which left her in that state for many years. My mom was the only one who took care of her.

It was heartbreaking to have to get her out of her hospital bed and bring her in and out of the bathroom. It was a tough job even though I helped my mom by pulling her up from the bed and helping her on and off the toilet bowl. So, with my mom being divorced and not having any help from my dad as far as no child support because he just took off, as if he had no responsibility whatsoever. To this day he doesn't care to know that he has two children, myself and my brother, we are seven years apart. I never met my grandfather because I was too young, I never had the opportunity to meet him. He had a very successful construction company and became very wealthy. He had built almost half the block with apartment buildings. After he had completed the buildings, he basically told my mom that she was to have one of the homes as a wedding gift prior to her getting married. Too many things had happened because it was so many years later, but I will tell the story the way it happened. When I was thirteen-years-old my mom remarried and I was not happy with her decision so when she did her and her husband continued to live with my grandmother until one day when my aunt came to my mother and stated that it would be a good idea for us to move back into the home I was born in, so in fact we moved out and moved back into that original house.

Nothing like moving back and forth a few times. Soon after my aunt started taking care of my grandmother she became very ill then passed on. I always found it strange to call it my opinion she made her sick. At this time my aunt had problems paying the taxes on that house, so she took out a second mortgage on my mom's house across the street for about eighty thousand dollars and made my mom pay back every dime to her for living there. Now by this time mom's husband was battling colon and liver cancer and not doing well.

After my mom spoke to several attorneys later, their advice to her was she had seven against her and didn't stand a chance at winning. The original will was changed in which stated that each child would receive after death that they would inherit money and properties but left my mom out of her inheritance they took her money and then told her she needed to leave the block altogether so again we had to pack up and moved into a small apartment in Nutley, NJ. Soon after mom's husband passed always from cancer. Right after I graduated high school back in 1986.They had been married for five years. From then on, I took care of my mom because her health started to deteriorate. At the time, my brother had moved out with an old girlfriend, so it was just me and my mom. After I graduated high school my mom and my brother purchased a townhouse in Clifton, NJ which is where I still reside with my brother. So, you may ask, "How can a family be so mean to a sister?" I have no answer. I guess there are rotten people who are just plain evil. Her brothers and sisters had no regard to how my mom felt about this and it grieved her for many years until her death. My mom was truly heartbroken with the way her own family treated her. Before she passed, she told me and my brother that if anything ever happened to her not to ever let them, meaning her family, come to her funeral and we did just that. There is no reason for a family to steal your money and not give you what was rightfully hers, but this is the whole truth to what happened.

The truth of the matter is this I was raised with the upmost respect for people however I have not run into any of my mom's family to this day, and if I did, I'm not sure what I would say. I choose to just move on and not let it bother me. I have my own life now anyway. I can only protect what's mine and make sure that no one ever could throw me out of my house or any house. In today's world you cannot trust just anyone. This is a reason enough to trust in Jesus that He will have His provision for our lives in His hands.

On another note, I have been going back and forth to doctors like cardiology and neurology along with primary care. My recent visits to the cardiologist meant me having to have another stress test and an echo cardio test. They both came back good with no problems with the heart, however my cholesterol is high, so my doctor has insisted that I start taking statin medicine for three months. I must do what the doctors say this time. I also am scheduled to have lidocaine injections in my neck for my migraines within the next few weeks. I will be seeing my pain management doctor at the end of the month to get a letter for my pending case. So, I have been running around a lot the past six months. I am trying to get all my medical records to my attorney so we can move forward.

I went online to read my stats and it stated it takes an average of 163 days for SSA to be decided. That will take me to the end of August 2021. I'm continually praying for God's will in my life and that He will work this all out in my favor. Hopefully, without going back to the court. I am planning on getting my passport this summer too. I'm also thinking of cancelling my gym membership at Planet Fitness because I'm getting tired of being in that type of environment. When this gym opened it was great and only a few blocks away, but the atmosphere has changed unfortunately for the worse so I'm debating joining another gym. Possibly, Blink but I have not made up my mind yet. I have always worked out. I don't lift heavy weights like I used to in my twenties, but I can still do strength training and cardio. I started working out when I was seventeen years old, so I am in good health so far. I can no longer have dairy and meat because of the cholesterol being high and now being on meds for it now for a few months until September 2021.

The stress factor isn't helping me so I will continue to be in prayer with that too. I tell the truth if it wasn't for God in my life there would be no way that I could have gone through half of what I did in my life. I give Him complete trust and confidence that He will make all things possible for me. One night I was sleeping, and I woke up about three in the morning and I felt the spirit telling me that Jesus wants me to let Him represent me and that He will go before me just like when He will go before me to his Father. He is my representative I just have to follow His lead and not talk h will speak up for me concerning all the things in my life. He also told me that He is going to begin to open windows and doors of blessings for me, and that I should be on the lookout for those occurrences to start happening. I can honestly say that I'm very filled with the spirit of God and sometimes He must wake me up in the wee hours of the morning to get my attention because He knows that's when I can hear Him clearly so every now and again, He gives me advice and a word.

I like to commune with Him that way too when everyone is asleep. After that is when I fall back to sleep. It's amazing but that's my secret between me and Jesus. On an average I hear from Jesus when I'm most stressed out and have no one to talk to about my problems and He does hear my cries and He knows my inner most thoughts and worries, in which He does talk to me about my worrying that it's not healthy for me, but He does understand because my mom was a huge worrier. I'm trying so hard not to but, in this case, sometimes it's extremely difficult and a lot easier said than done. In my weakness He is my strength. Amen. No matter what storm I am in I still remain to praise him in the storm, and I will lift my hands because I know who he is. My help comes from the Lord. If it hadn't been for Him, I don't know where I would have wound up. I can't thank Him enough for the things he has brought me through.

When I was at church one morning, I had went to the connect desk to inquire about membership to my church and to be considered for the music ministry so they gave me a packet with four CD's to listen to along with the actual application questionnaire and at the bottom of the page it asked for two referrals from a leader or pastor/staff to sign it so I got in touch with one of my leaders from my old church I used to attend and that I was with for years to sign it for me and I are to get one more signature then hand it back to the church for reviews. I'm still praying on this as well for me to part of something where my heart's desire is to sing for God and to give Him all the praise His deserves. God's will in my life is what I desire to unfold His plan for me. As He knows the plans He has for me.

Things are starting to get tough about now as though I am being attacked because I am trying to move in a direction in which the devil doesn't like at all. Let me explain it was. On Memorial Day and I was scheduled to see a certain nurse practitioner about getting a recent MRI reading that was ordered by this person. I was instructed to go to this Riverside medical building so when I got there I went inside and was immediately refused to be seen they had told me that because I had changed my primary care physician I wouldn't be seen unless I called my insurance company and have it transferred over back to Riverside Medical. I said, "No way will I do that." I then left the building as I informed them; I was there to see this person to consult with her. But this wasn't going to happen. I then went downstairs and then left that office. I was so agitated at this point that I wanted nothing else to do with this practice again. I did try to tell them I was a patient of the pain management for over four years, but they said "you're not a patient here" which was very confusing to me since I still have dealings with this practice for my cardiology as well as pain management but because my doctor left the office in which I was treated was no longer there any longer. So, it left me stuck without a pain management doctor. Come to find out that this doctor opened a new practice and doesn't take Medicaid any longer, which was even worse. I said to myself, *I'm batting a thousand let's keep going now.*

I am waiting for my neurologist to call me with the appointment for me to come in and get the injections of lidocaine in my neck in two weeks. Prior to my scheduled appointment I decided to call to confirm this only to find out that they didn't do their job on getting the approval until 3:00 in the afternoon on a Friday. As it turned out I now must wait another two weeks only because one person didn't get the approval in on time. In the meantime, I'm still getting migraines and relying on my medications to subside. I'm battling every week now sometimes two times a week now. During that same week I had another MRI of the cervical neck, and I am waiting for the report to be typed up and read by the radiologist.

The medical system is way more than just broken and slow, I'm finding the employees who are in this field have lost the will to care about doing a job because in my opinion they have gotten too relaxed in the workplace nor do they remember to care about the patients. To have more patience at this pace is more of what I need at this present time in my life. Sometimes, I get so frustrated, and it feels as if I'm losing all my patience more and more nowadays. But in my weakness my God is there to remind me of His grace and mercy. I thank Him for that every day. It's not easy, what I'm saying you will find I'm more patient than I thought. That's why I must keep stretching myself, I keep telling myself a little longer. Soon this will all be over. When reaching to get someplace and it seems as though time is just standing still and you're not seeing any result on an expectation, your best thing to do is absolutely nothing. Just stand firm in the promises of God. He does promise He will give strength to the weak and in your weakness, He becomes your innermost strength. I live by faith and not by sight. Even if I cannot see the result in whatever it is I'm searching for doesn't mean he isn't working behind the scenes.

As we approach Memorial Day weekend, things have been heating up and I'm not talking about just the weather I'm talking about my need to get things done on my own and not rely on the medical staff in theses doctor offices, since my pain management doctor left the practice, it hasn't been a joy with getting anything from them in regards to making an appointment with them because they don't have another doctor in that building. To make a long story short, I continued to see my neurologist and I did get the injections in my head just a few days ago. That night the injections sites hurt a little bit but nothing like what I expected. That Friday night I was able to attend my church service. After the service, I had to give a message to my pastor that someone told me to say "hello" to him, so I did just that. During that day, I had attended a viewing of my last pastor in whom had passed away last Saturday and was being laid out in the church I was practically raised up in all through my teen and young adult years, so I had to pay my respects. I also reached out to another pastor that I knew when I was a child and from the first church I was saved, and water baptized in to have him sign my referral sheet for the second signature for that form. I mailed it to him and put a self-addressed envelope with the form so he can return it to me. After it's completely signed, I will, as promised, give it to my church and continue to proceed with getting membership and get into the music ministry. I will let the Holy Spirit lead and guide me with the rest. I've been making so much progress I managed to get my passport pictures taken and I scheduled my appointment to get a new passport. I'm moving forward with this and doing all I need to do to get ready for my breakthrough and for me to start my travels very soon. I'm looking forward to starting over again with life now that I am fully vaccinated. I am going to get on a plane and head to Florida to see my longtime friends Lynn and Kenny. We are going to have a great time. I also will be looking forward to eventually cruising as well.

I'm finished with getting more documents for my attorney. I would like to drop by her office to give her my files so she can make copies of everything I have for my case. So, in fact I did just that although she was out of the office and working from home, like everyone else.

I figured that if I can give my files for the past five years plus then there won't be any room for mistakes this time. We now will have all the ammunition we will need if it goes that far. Then at that point I would have said I gave it my all with no details left out. After I handed the file case over, I felt as if I did the last of the last things that I could do. It's in God's hands, too.

I will be planning my vacation soon, my appointment for passport has been set and I had to save up money for this too, some things you must save for. Yes, the "Rainy Day." I never have a problem saving money for a purpose. That's always been one of my strong points. I'm not the kind of person who likes to live paycheck to paycheck but being forced into this can be very difficult to do for the most part. We all had dreams, hopes, and plans in America, we call it having the American Dream. You work hard to save money, take care of the family and all come together for Sunday dinner and if you did it right you can take a vacation once a year. Oh boy, have times changed, in the 21st century people can't afford anything of the sort now and it literally takes two people to pay the bills in the home.

I was taught at a young age that you work hard and save your money until you can't work any longer were my mom's favorite words for me. She knew all about my back problems including the pain she saw me go through for years. Well, that time has initially come,

I cannot work anymore due to the chronic pain. I did enjoy working as a cashier at both Kohl's and Target stores. I also had the opportunity to work for Macy's a few years back. I have to say Jesus had my life in His hands the whole time. He always provided me with every job I've ever had.

This is why He will always be my Jehovah Jirah. He always opened the right doors at the right time, so if it's one thing that I know it is this, "God doesn't sleep. He's always on time and never late." Never take advantage of that. The Lord speaks through the Holy Spirit to you in a still small voice "Trust in the Lord and lean not unto your own understanding." By doing this, He will direct your path and that path will lead you to your destiny. So maybe you have questions on how will He or how do I know what my destiny is? Well, the answer is clear, walk in your ways, be righteous before Him, (meaning be in right standing) be in His will for your life and you will be directed into the right direction and calling for your life. By doing this and continuing being in the Word and in constant prayer to the father who does hear our supplications every time. He does require one thing before blessing or cursing and that one thing is obedience. Many of us are not obedient to the call of God on their life, and that is a huge reason why things sometimes go the opposite direction, and their life seems so scattered and out of control.

Too many times in the hustle and bustle of this life we forget to acknowledge that Jesus is there all the time listening and waiting to hear a word from us. Constant communication is key to having the joy of the Lord in your life. Now I'm not saying that once you lay your life at the feet of Jesus that everything is going to be perfection not at all, it takes commitment to build your relationship with the Lord and knowledge and great wisdom to commune with God every day. Most may choose to say, "Hey I'm a good person therefore I should be allowed into heaven when I pass." But this is an ignorant mind frame because it's something like this. Would you allow someone who wants nothing to do with you, doesn't talk to you, or is even nice to you to be welcome into your home? Well, think of heaven that way the only way of getting in is if you are born again and in communication of your repentance with Jesus which means do you have a personal relationship with Him? Because if you don't it may be very difficult for you to try to get in and most likely you won't. The Bible states in John (3:3) Jesus is very clear on this. There is no way around this and certainly no compromise. The choice is totally yours that's what Jesus meant when He said, "Choose Life," because He is Life. If you do you will have everlasting eternal life. We all don't think of the afterlife too often but there is a real Heaven as much as a real Hell. Jesus promises to go and prepare a place for "Us" if we do follow him. That Bible verse is found in John (14:2-3).

During Covid-19 we lost a lot of lives, some lost a mom or a dad, brother, sister, cousin or in some cases best friends. We all know someone, and I can't stress enough how important it is to just give thanks to God that every day we walk, live, and have breath in our lungs to give Thanks and Praise for everyday is a blessing. I'm surely blessed to just know Him and am so grateful. Not every day is perfect, things may not go as we plan, but... at least we have a day one more than others. I just personally want to get involved in all that I can in the house of the Lord especially in these times. I am moving forward with getting involved with the ministry as I will also be learning to play the guitar for the first time in my life. Of course, there is a protocol in becoming a member of the church in which I am currently doing. I handed in the questionnaire with the names of two leaders of mine who signed the document for me on my behalf. After doing so I emailed my attorney regarding my pending case and she told me, "I should be hearing something soon from SSA." I know that everything is being worked out in the heavens for me and I will have everything in His time. I've been applying for low-income apartments with the hopes that I will hear of one soon. I've been on waiting lists for the past few years. I've received some letters back but none which I qualified for. I didn't meet the yearly minimum requirements for some of the apartments. This is where faith and trust come into play because, even though I don't see this in the natural doesn't mean it's not there in the supernatural. I do feel that there is one that has my name on it already. All part of the plan for my life. It's all going to come together nicely real soon I can feel it in my spirit and my innermost being.

Here we are during summer. It's July already, we blink and the months a just fly by. Things are starting to move in the right direction for me such as me becoming a member within my church. I had my interview on a Monday in July. I also started taking lessons in singing and playing the guitar on Friday nights before the service. That same week I was able to hand in my passport application to the post office. So, I would like to keep seeing things open for me, as the floodgates of Heaven open as well. It's been a rough winter and I'm looking forward to going on my vacation this year to Lake George for the first time in August of 2021.

Right now, I'm in a better place emotionally than before. I'm less stressed but still am battling with some anxiety and do need just a little more patience which I'm working on each day. If someone were to ever ask me, "What gets you through all the tough times?" I'd have to honestly tell them that I pray every day and night and read my Bible regularly even if it's a few verses at a time. I've been reading the Book of Revelation regularly with a study Bible. I find that a study Bible is easiest to understand because it breaks the verses down for you in simpler terms.

I'm also getting ready for the women's conference at my church next week July 24, 2021. Each year, I look forward to this time because it brings me closer to the Lord spiritually and the best part is there are no men there, it's just women! It's more of a time of praise and worship. I'm expecting it to be awesome.

"The best is yet to come" some say, however that may be just a figure of speech, but I say it is very optimistic and that's what I'm saying it is going to be for this year. I think that I am due for a very serious jubilee in my near future, and a time well deserved! I will wait upon the Lord and ask that He renew my strength in the meantime to work this all out for me for my hearing. I will not give up. I will continue to fight the good fight of faith with tooth and nail and see until I see the victory. "How do I do that?" You may ask. My response is simple, "In prayer." I fought all my battles in prayer with the scriptures in my mouth and I spoke to them day and night. At times, I had to fight negative with rebuke and pick up the armor and take my stand for what God promised me. He never tells us we wouldn't go through trials but what he does say is when we do go through them, He will be with us during those hard trials, and when we go through the fire he will be there. Even when we go through the valley of death, He will be right there to meet us. The fact is the trials build your character and make your faith rise higher and stronger than ever before. Without them you stay stagnant, and you don't grow spiritually. Jesus will never leave us or forsake us, even in our darkest hours that's His promise to each one of us. He also tells us not to be anxious about anything, and that we should also make our requests known to Him in prayer. This verse is in Philippians (4:6) along with a promise that He clearly stated in (Rom.8:28) we know that all things work together, for good to those who love God, to those who are called according to His purpose. So, in the end it all works out for His Glory.

Now, at a time such as this, with a deadly virus on the rise again and again, we stand a very slight chance of coming out of this without catching this illness. I have been vaccinated but more importantly each day it's important to cover yourself with The Blood of Jesus. You may ask "what is that?" It is my pleasure to tell what exactly that means in a biblical sense. Each day in your "prayers" to the Lord, you ask Him to cover you with His blood, and His Robe of righteousness and plead His blood over your life, to protect you from all things. Read Psalms 91 too. I always pray this way and for His protection pray a hedge of thorns around you every day. What this does it puts a barrier around you against the enemy that nothing can come near you. Praying building hedges also should be done in the most secret places of prayer. This also builds a hedge against doors of weakness that may attack you with all sorts of temptations. This was taught to me at a very young age to pray this way. I've learned a lot being brought up in a church that was on fire for God. Holy Spirit filled sermons three times a week you can learn a lot. Talking about letting the fire fall and letting the Holy Spirit flow during a worship service in praise is unlike anything you can ever experience. It's about being in God's presence that has truly impacted my whole life's purpose.

"Purpose" is all what I describe as the real reason why we were created. We were all created for worship and to worship God. It's that simple, yes... we all have our hopes and dreams in this life but when this life is gone our worship to the Lord will always be within our souls. This is why we have a soul. He made us to be immortal beings, yes but, the soul leaves our human body and goes to our destination. Heaven or Hell. With that being said, the soul is the life principle of a human being the immortal element of man the (inner man) the spirit the living individual. This is stating that when we pass away, we are at that moment absent from the body and present with the Lord.

It's important to know that we do have a purpose in life. Life is much more than just working hard and paying the bills to just live the normal life. You can have money and all the riches this world has to offer; however, nothing is compared to the promises of God and what He has in store for those who love Him and truly want to have a relationship with him. He promised to give us the Holy Spirit as our helper till the end of "time." The return of his second coming.

In my previous writings I have on many occasions spoke about my personal life and the rest of the story, which is at hand, which is why I decided to write this book was because I wanted whoever chooses to read this would be blessed and inspired by the actual events that took place in one's lifetime. The fact that I have persevered through every obstacle and hurdle didn't mean that I never thought I would but that my greatest accomplishment was that Jesus as with me through it "all." I don't have a red carpet under my feet and wasn't born with a silver spoon in my mouth, but what I do have is a good attitude no matter what the circumstance was and a grateful heart. A heart after God. So, I can stand in his throne room one finds day and look forward to having him say "well done my faithful child" and welcome me into the kingdom of Heaven. Those who know me in a personal way and who are in my inner circle would testify that I have a good sense of humor and even if I'm dealing with an impossible situation that I would always get myself out of it and rise above it.

To get to the particulars and to elaborate on current events such as me getting into the music ministry with the church I attend, well that didn't happen. I received a phone call and was informed that my voice does have potential but not at this moment in time. They also suggested that I can take up singing lessons to strengthen the voice, which would teach me techniques. My reply was "okay" what else can I say? It's not like I'm going to jump ship because I didn't get to fulfill my calling. I'm still a member and I am doing administration work there. The thing is sometimes some things are harder than others to accept. God says either "YES,""NO," "WAIT…" Never maybe! Patience is a must. So, that's what I must do is move on. I'm getting ready for my court hearing in two weeks anyway. I cannot be distracted any more than I have already been the past few weeks. What I mean by that is the late nights that I can't fall asleep and waking up very nervous and having panic attacks is the best way I can describe my mental wellbeing. I can hear the still small voice inside me saying "Be Still and Know that I am God." Every night I'm calling out to Jesus just to calm me down. I can feel as the time gets closer the pressure on me. I am praying for peace also in my time of need. I know deep inside God is faithful, and He would have never put me on a path that he wouldn't see me through. The heart knows better but the stuff that goes on in your head is where the real battle is. It's a constant fight, and I'm fighting this one to the end. So, the date is set for my hearing and after its all said and done, I'm planning on taking a long vacation from thinking about anything from then on. I have visions of a warm beach and blue water too and not to mention looking at palm trees in sunny Florida. This is my desire, and my desire is to dream. To be continued as they say...

Chapter 10

The only thing I would like to see is that you pay close attention to the details of what I am about to describe in the next few pages. I believe this was truly coming to me straight from the spirit.

This is for the person who every morning gets up out of bed and puts the coffee on while sitting at their kitchen table and stares at the trees outside. Season after season with and without the leaves on its branches as they bow their "heads" in prayer to the Almighty and says, "God, where am I going to get money to pay for food and my car payments, or my insurance this week?" As the weeks turn into months and the months into years they continue to slowly move as time waits for no one or nothing, oh "Where will I get help from? Please send help! I don't know where else to turn as I'm so overwhelmed with this grief over the waiting. I can barely breathe. Then just as I take a sip of my hot coffee, I can hear the voice of my Father saying, "Do not fear my child, I'm with you." "Be still and know that I am God. I have set you on a path and ordained your steps to move forward which will lead you into your victory!" Amen.

My friend, I promise you it'll be worth it all to give God all the glory and the honor for the things He has done in my life and in someone else's as well. What He has done for me, He will surely do for you. Hold true to your faith in Jesus like never before, grab onto His garment where power flows. Stay in the spirit and walk in love, forgiving one another from grace and mercy above. It's all there we just need to be humble at His feet, so that when we fall, He can pick us up off our knees. Soon enough we will see Him face to face, "Oh my God, I cannot wait..." Will I dance for you Jesus? or "to my knees will I fall?" I can only imagine what it will be like in heaven and the angels before you fall singing "Glory Hallelujah Raise the banner high" this Ones coming home please don't deny. We've made our way, opened the gate carried them through all this way just to see you.

They travelled so far and few with no one around them only but you, they trusted in your everlasting love that you freely gave, even ran with it every single day, they honored you with all that they did and say and though their life they struggled hardship and strife but never once did they lose faith for their life.

We stand before your Heavenly Throne asking you for entrance to your home? And a well-deserved welcome for this child truly loved the Lord with all their heart and soul. Grant them oh so many blessings that only heaven can afford and send to them rewards and crowns that they patiently waited for. Send kisses from above and sun from the sky to the ones down below who always cry wipe their tears away as you dry their eyes. Fill their hearts with joy and compassion. For the lost for this is our prayer to our Lord and Savior of the World. Amen.

On this journey from life to home as we know it, everything that happens does happen for a reason even if we don't understand how or why. In this lifetime we will see setbacks, comebacks, delays and forthcomings, however we choose to have or gain perspective on the situations is all how to perceive it. We don't even think about how many times in a single day that a delay at a traffic light can be the miracle of something that God saved us from on the other side of the block or down the street. It may have been an accident that could have been you but we were stuck at the long traffic light complaining about it. Or being in line at the grocery store longer than we wanted to be there only to find out about a catastrophe waiting outside. God delays us for his reason to protect us, but we pay no mind to it because we are so self-absorbed.

Timing sometimes isn't like our time, we want things done by our watch and God doesn't use watches or clocks, so we need to learn we are on his timeline.

Know this that when He does answer your prayers it will be his time in his way. This is where He tests our patience. He will test our patience every day until we get it right. Just when we think we are patient, do we find out when we go through trials and tribulations that we don't have any patience at all. I thought I had so much patience only to find out I didn't have enough, and I needed to really work on that. One example of that was when my attorney called me to tell me my court date was moved up a week. On the contrary, the fact that I've been waiting for five years I had to wait longer than I anticipated, which sent me into a state of mind questioning "Why?" All I can think of was when is this case going to be over and finished with so that I can get on with my life. So, this is where I had to take a breath and say, "One more week. I have no control over this now do I?" Not all things are in our control. I have learned to let go and let God take over now and moving forward. Yes, I have learned this the hard way, thinking that if I worried myself sick it would make a difference, but it doesn't matter, in fact it makes things much worse. This was a learning experience for me personally. The outcome is much greater than the problem. Just as finding a solution to a problem is far better than doing nothing than explaining it over and over to everyone as if they really understand. I'm so thankful that Jesus knows me and understands me even at my worst. He sees and hears everything, including my thoughts.

In my therapy sessions, my therapist tells me that I need to find ways to capture my negative thoughts before they come. Although this is very hard to do at times, I have been getting much better at doing this. The conversation would start something like this. "How are you feeling today?" or "How would you say your mood is today?" My reply would be, "I feel…" meaning whatever I felt that morning or what my emotions felt at that moment from events that happened during the week. Most of the time I would say, "I felt horrible or depressed or just moody, just not in a good mood." Whatever the reasoning would be for me not feeling good was contrary to why I needed therapy. I was in therapy for a few years because I needed someone to generally to talk me through me of the things that I have a hard time adjusting too. It also is good to vent to someone who doesn't know you and won't judge you the way your friends would or even family members would. At the end of each session, she would ask me, "Did you find anything interesting about today's conversation?" I would have to answer and say, "Yes, I did thanks for being here for me just to talk with." The thing I like about this is the opinions of friends are almost always going to be partial to me and I need brutal honesty. That is what I like about therapy. She tells me the way it is if I like it or not. Whereas most friends don't want to hurt your feelings, so they are afraid to be completely honest with you about sensitive subjects.

There is another factor in place that has crossed my mind on several occasions; you go to church, or would

I consider doing that? I ask myself that sometimes. But I rather not do that only because I don't want to bring any attention to myself by unloading my stuff like that on the church that I attend. Maybe just because I don't think anyone would be able to relate. Some things are better left between "us" and the Lord. In the Bible, its states, "Cast your burdens upon Him for He will sustain you. He shall never permit the righteous to be moved. Psalms (55:22). The word "Cast" would refer to throw out. As if you're going to throw your fishing rod out to sea to fish metaphorically speaking this illustrates taking your cares or burdens and throwing them on Jesus. He wants them all of it. After and during your times of casting your burdens to the Lord in prayer the next step is not to be moved. While you wait upon God, it's important to worship while we wait. Serve Him while we wait even though it may not be easy, but it is a key point, and detrimental to our walk with the Lord. Know that during this time this will be when He will put our "patience" to the test. There aren't enough words to express how many times my patience has been tested time and time again. But in that I've been able to build character, because that is what it does it rebuilds character into the person, he wants you to become.

I'm going to be celebrating my fifty-fourth birthday on February 3rd, and I am so blessed to be able to do that. I will be enjoying it because this one is going to be a good one with more blessings than I can ever imagine. I'm so grateful and thankful that I came this far and that my dreams and goals are still in process. This wish will be for me to have all the things that I need in my life to go according to God's will in my life. I will also wish for a financial windfall to come into my life. "Breakthrough" is the better way of saying it. I always love getting gifts too, especially "cosmetics." I don't have to know what they are I just know that I like getting them. Every year, I blow out my candles and expect to hear good news and I haven't had good news regarding my case, but this year will be different. I know that God is faithful to me, and He has a plan for me. I just must let Him do His job now. I heard recently from a pastor on TV say one time, "Let go and let God." Makes sense to me because we ask Him to do something for us, we surrender it to Him and still want to take control over the thing, but if we don't move out of the way and take a back seat how can He take it from us completely when we are still holding onto it? I'm not going to say that I haven't done this time and time again, but we all have come short of the Glory of God. I'm personally working on that. Taking it before the Lord in prayer. Hopefully you will too.

The time is getting close to my court hearing I have exactly two weeks and I'm holding on to the promise that Jesus will come through for me. On February 7,

2022, the Bible verse that just happened to be for that day specifically was (Jeramiah 29:11). This is the verse I've been standing on for the past five years and pertained to me, because this was the day my mom went home to be with Jesus in 2012. You never forget no matter how many years go by, it's just one of those things that sticks with you. Always remembering dates and times, events and occurrences. It's something how your brain doesn't put that stuff someplace far away like in another compartment.

The human brain is designed that way that it literally puts what we don't want to remember in our subconscious mind. That's why from time to time we will be reminded of something from our past and it shows up in all different kinds of ways. Could be good or bad but in some cases, we may have heard that it can manifest itself in a dream or a vision. I'd like to take a few minutes and talk about "vision." I know that most people would say, "What does that mean?" The word "vision" can be used in different ways. In the Bible, it means to be able to have it means to be able to see in the supernatural, by this example would be to say that we all need to be able to see more for ourselves or have such as Faith that we can see things that are already there even when they are not in the flesh. Another example would be to vision what the future holds for you. Insight. We all need to have spiritual vision to what God has called you to do, and or how can one be a service to him. We need to be seeking first the kingdom and all things will be added. That simply means seek God first and He will give you the desires of your hearts but not until we make him our priority in life. So, ask yourself this question. What do you vision for your own life? What do you think God would be saying to you today? "Search my heart, Lord. See if I'm doing your will according to your purpose that I may be pleasing you." This we should meditate on it day and night so that we are in His will for our lives. Take time out and pray for Him to show you and I believe He will.

Chapter 11

The title for this book, *Anchored*, came to me very early on as a quick word to my spirit and I just went with it. However, I thought about exactly what that meant to me, and it's been a great pleasure to bring this to you now in full circle. Over the next few pages, I will describe what this meant to me personally and hope it finds you well. As I have mentioned in the first few pages, while I was on a luxurious cruise with Royal Caribbean the idea of writing this book came across to me as I laughed and said, "What? Can I really do this?" Questioning as I was giggling all the way through my lunch. I nearly fell off the bench I was sitting on, and I replied to my dear friend who was sitting with me and said, "You know I'm going to do it; I don't know where or how but I'm going to proceed at some point to start writing." And so here I am… at the finish line. Just running the race to write something captivating enough to get the attention of someone in need of something more than just the average self-help book. Let me explain…

To first know what an anchor does, it holds the ship so that when it's time to dock it doesn't move. Now there is a lot to be said about this in biblical terms such as this life or journey we will have storms that we will go through. During those storms, when the waves seem to become overbearing as if it feels like you're going to drown and drift away, the anchor is what holds you in place so that you don't drift away. That Anchor is "Jesus." The Anchor is dropped way down deep into the waters into the sand. What that means to us is we should dig down into the word of God. Dig deep into it so that we don't drift away from Him. When the storms of life hit you, we are to worship more because that's where He is found in the hardship and in our lowest places at the lowest times of our lives. When I say "drifted" it can mean be tempted far into temptation and most of the time we don't see it coming, it just sort of happens we find ourselves distancing ourselves away from God like sand through our fingers and the things of God. There are so many factors that can take place to distract us in a single day even, so we are not to disassemble ourselves from God. Attach yourself to that Anchor to be sure steadfast because in that same Anchor is the courage to try again and not lose ground and to keep moving forward no matter what happens. It's an anchor of hope in that knowing God is for me not against me. He is the anchor of my soul that nothing can separate us from the love of God because we are forever attached. Amen.

Now ask yourself this important question "Are you anchored in Jesus?" If not, do you want to be? Do you want Him to be the captain of your ship and your life? If so, then I would like for you to allow me to help you by inviting Jesus into your heart and life today. Now you can pray this simple prayer to yourself or out loud either way he will hear you. Say these words:

> *Father, in the name of Jesus, I come to you now and I ask you to forgive me of all my sins and wash me clean. I believe that you sent your only Son to die on a cross for me so that I may be saved, and I want Jesus to be Lord of my life. Come into my heart and fill me with your spirit. In Jesus's name I pray. Amen.*

Now if you just prayed that prayer, I do believe you are saved. All your sins are washed away, and you are a new creation in Jesus. Get into a Bible-based church and read the Bible daily as you continue your walk with the Lord. This has been the best choice that you will ever make for your entire life. God Bless.

Now the final stage begins, the fight of the ages, here I am at the very finish line of my five-year fight for my social security disability case. I'm going to tell you exactly how this round went. The stage was set, and the players were standing in center range. On the front lines were my attorney, the judge, and myself and most of all- my defender JESUS Himself. The devils were there ready to take me down as well, but God said, "No way. Not on my clock not this one." God turned His head, looked down from heaven and said, "My Son, what do you have to say?" Jesus looks up and says, "My daughter, I've known her since her birth she has had a terrible childhood she came to me since she was seven and I raised her up to call her my own. I was her father because she was fatherless, and she was a caretaker to her mother." This child is the very apple of my eye and the rarest of the gems. She has been through so many things time and time again from broken relationships which left her abandoned and done in, I felt favor on her and gave her mercy to live her life again. She has suffered tremendous amounts of loss and yet still praised me from deep within. She continued praying and making her requests known without a single day of knowing the outcome. She trusted in Me." Then God lifts His head and says, "Go ahead make her day!"

The stage was set the questions started one by one and I answered just as I was told. They went through my life's history without missing a beat, making sure they got all the information which would leave grounds for defeat. Then just when I thought it was going in a different direction and could hear the devils counting down to the wire from ten to zero it was over. I got off the phone more devastated as I can be, not knowing what happened thought I lost everything, I bowed my head in shame and just as the last tear fell from my eyes the God of my salvation broke through with my phone ringing and me not hearing it on the line was my attorney herself telling me the final word, "I WON!" I screamed, "Oh my GOD! THANK YOU! Did I really do this? I really won my case?" She replied "YES!" I couldn't believe my ears it was all over. She told me the judge approved me before I get on the line while I was in the waiting room awaiting my hearing to begin. I couldn't stop praising Jesus for that all day long. I'm so grateful and thankful for a prayer answered. The devil lost. Defeated. All his tricks and torments he tried to put me through he's been defeated, and Jesus is the winner and so am I. For in the word, it says "We are more than conquerors through Jesus who loved us." (Romans 8:37).

It's been a few days since getting this huge victory and I'm still waiting for the initial documentations that need to be filled out to close out my case for me to be finished with the process. But overall, it is over. I do feel much better but am still going through the feelings of extreme tiredness. I will be looking forward to the next phase of life.

As I look back as far as I can still remember, I will never forget God's faithfulness to me. I'm going to take you back to very specific times where He has provided for me in ways that are unexplainable. In 2017, when I realized that I couldn't continue working with the back pain that I was going through, and it was at that point I knew it was going to cause me a great deal of problems.

So, I had no choice but to go on a temporary disability for six months. I was only working for that company for nine months. When I went to my human resource department, I was informed that I wasn't there long enough to even get any sort of compensation.

However, Jesus interceded where that was His concern. After a month or so I was able to get paid for my medical leave. The very next thing that I had to deal with was that I had a car lease which was about to end and so I was put into a very difficult situation. Not knowing what to do I was about to lose my car and my only means of transportation, until I had a conversation with the owner of the dealership in which I was a loyal customer, said to me, "If you ever need anything come see me, I value you as a longstanding customer." Well, the time came, and I can still recall walking into the dealership one day and I asked to speak to him, he came out from the office, and I asked if he could help me out because my lease wasn't up, yet and I wasn't going to be able to keep the payment due to the fact I didn't have enough income. He then right then and there had me sit with his general manager and took that car out of my hands and put me into a new car for less money than I was paying. God's grace once again. He showed me favor and provision. It came to the point that I needed to find out how I can get food. So, one day I just went onto my laptop and searched government programs, and I came across a program that I can apply for food. That was called SNAP. Along with medical general assistance with some cash. As I was assigned an appointment to go to social services, I did all that I could do to try to help myself in getting the necessities that I needed that life. Soon after that doors started to open for me with friends helping me every way they can. I had a dear friend introduce me to consumer product testing to make extra money. This came in just when I needed it too. The list continued from then on. It showed me that everything was going according to plan.

My friend I'm here to tell you that when you find yourself in a situation where you don't know what to do next, simply bow your head in pray for God to help you. It's that easy when you don't know what to ask or even how just to say "Help." He is faithful to do just that. He will provide for you in every way possible even when you can't. Just as when you look outside at the trees, do you see how the branches are stretched out toward the heavens? Look at the birds in the sky, they aren't worried about where they will eat and sleep. As far as the oceans deep although you cannot see the "depth," but you know that God created it. The mountains reach as high into the heavens as it shouts out "Glory." His creation alone in interweaving a baby in the mother's womb is a miracle so every time you hear a baby cry or a puppy bark even a cat meow. Remember He made them all. He created us with His miracle working "hands." Think of it this way when you pray, and you give it to Jesus let it go. Continue praying without ceasing.

When things get so out of control remember that when you prayed you asked the Lord to take it from you and He did. He took all that you asked and all the tears you cried out of your hands and into His hands. For those are where the miracles happen, and you will see His hands at work. To fulfill all His purposes and promises in your life, just as He did for me.

This book goes out to my one true love who never left me wanting for anything and has shown me to be more faithful than I can ever imagine. His love, mercy, and grace. Encouragement beyond measures. His patience reaches far beyond the deepest sea. He has been closer than a best friend and remains a "King." His Glory is splendor, and it radiates through the sun his name is YESHUA-JESUS GOD'S ONLY SON. Amen.

Chapter 12

This chapter is called, "The Enemy and His Plots." We live in a world where the enemy is on the move all the time. I mean he really does roam to and from the earth like a slithering snake, seeking whom he may destroy. The thing is we as Christians cannot give him any room to move, or as I call it wiggle room in your heart, or your life. Just as Jesus has plans for us to prosper and fulfill our own calling on our lives the enemy works harder to attack you, and he literally plans out plots to make sure he uses whatever he can to distract you, "and for what?" Is the big question? The answer to that is… he wants to stop you from entering the presence of God. The more you enter the Holy of Holies the closer you get to God the further God will lead you into your true calling, and that will ultimately lead you into the perfect will for your life. This is why is very important to be on alert and not to let your guard down. Be fired up, prayed up always ready to fight back and get ready to crush the enemy.

Some examples of what I am referring to I will explain by giving you clips of certain scenarios that took place for me personally on my journey. Going back a few years ago while I was pending my court case to be finalized, the timeline was excruciating for me, and I had to seriously get before the Lord every day and ask for patience and perseverance. There came a point in time that I had to totally trust in Him and that it would all work out. However, during the whole time, the enemy tried everything he could to distract me from truly entering the true presence of God. I would worship and praise every day, but he tried so hard by putting negative thoughts into my head. He would whisper things like "What if it doesn't go the way you want?" "What are you going to do then?" He would then fill my head with so many lies and torment me so that I would only keep my eyes on the circumstance and not on Jesus just so I would lose focus. Just like Peter on the water when he looked away from Jesus he started sinking under water. Until he regained his focus.

The more he would try this the more I had to praise and pray against this type of attack. Little did I know then what I know now that the thing that was my weakest area became my strongest defense now. God used that very thing to make me stronger and it taught me that I can put the enemy underneath my feet. The Bible speaks of this very clearly, and that we have the authority to stomp on the serpent and I did just that.

Another way he tried to distract me would be to get me so wound up over the whole situation where I would lose my focus and sometimes, I made the problem bigger than my faith. So again, when a problem bigger than you comes up in life, we must not make it bigger than it is by listening to the lies that the devil tells you. Always remember that God is bigger than your problem bigger than your situation and He can handle any situation that seems to be overpowering you. See, the enemy wants you to think that you're stuck, not going to get out, trapped, and even confined. But that's not the case at all. We have all freedom in Jesus and Liberty we all are set free in Him.

We are not bound by anything, especially the enemy with his tricks and plots. A key thing Jesus spoke to my sprint one night was this. When Jesus and His grace walk into a room all the things that seem impossible become possible.

At service the church is packed with praise and worship hands raised everyone singing praises as more people keep coming in and walking in front of me can't help but get distracted while they are looking for a seat. Late arrivers are another distraction. Because just when your eyes are closed you hear noises so you can't help but open them to see that someone is walking in front of you to get to a seat next to you. Another distracting thing is that it can be a person sitting next to you who constantly chooses to get your attention or talk to you while you're praising and worshiping Jesus during the worship time. The enemy uses all these small distractions so that you don't enter the presence of God. He uses people to carry out his theme for the night, so you get angry enough to stop what you're focusing on which was the Lord. So, what do you do when this happens? Ignore it, keep your eyes on the Lord anyway, don't let the enemy have your time, don't give in to His game. That's what it is to him it's a huge game so you lose focus and get distracted away from praising God. Put that devil under your feet, by praising anyway. Jesus deserves our undivided attention. If we aren't focused, we lose perspective on what the Holy Spirit may be trying to tell us, so it's important not to allow such instances to take control or have lead way in any area where your worship time can be interrupted. This can be another form of the devil manipulating you by making you feel somewhat guilty for not paying mind to him, so he gets agitated more then tries to hit you in another area. In your weakest areas, he sees an open door he will try to come in, but we must be aware of this when it does happen and remember where the attack originated from.

In speaking about praise, it's not optional. The Bible says that let everything that has breath praise the Lord. (Psalms 150:6). We are to praise God no matter what we may be going through. The good, the bad, the ups and the downs of this life we are to be joyfully praised. If we don't the rocks will praise him. Praise also gives your perspective. It's personal. The power of praise is a sign of your life. "Choose you this day will you serve?" Declare it because there is so much power behind praise.

Gas-lighting is another huge way of manipulation (psychological abuse) used by the enemy to have one's reality questioned by another. An easier way to explain this so that one may understand it this… You may have done something or said something to someone that wasn't the right thing to do or say so when you apologize the response from the other person has you questioning why you apologized in the first place. It makes you feel even worse than the incident that took place from the beginning. So therefore, you feel guilty about something you know you were right about the whole time. But now they gaslight you into thinking and questioning yourself. It's total abuse and very hurtful but the enemy knows what buttons to push so he will use this method to distract you from what we are taught.

"If you don't forgive someone's sins your Father in heaven won't forgive yours." (Matthew 6:15). Although this may be hard to do but we all must pray and seek the Lord for Him to help us deal with this in area of our lives because we all, at some point, have gone through it. Be strong and courageous know who you are in Christ Messiah, let the Holy Spirit guide your heart and listen to it, also and you won't be gaslit by anyone. The Bible states that we are as sheep and his sheep hear the voice of God. To hear the voice of God you must be still and mostly quiet to hear that still small whisper that will come in the times of being in the presence of God. Now there are many ways to hear God speak to you for example he may have you open your Bible, and it may be a word in there just pertaining to your current situation that you're in at that very moment in your life. He may speak to you in a song that you hear when you turn your radio on to your Christian music station on that you hear at that minute that you just needed to hear, and it really touches your heart.

There are many times in life when we will be going through something that doesn't seem fair or not right and we don't know what to do about the current situation. You may feel that God has gone away or seem so far from you that you cannot seem to find any answers to why our ship is sinking and we aren't setting sail as per say cruising. There are reasons for this, and I would like to enlighten you on this to help you. There are a few reasons why we are put into such circumstances, and I will be more than happy to explain and give you a much better perspective of what's really going on. In most cases, the number one problem for all the problems we encounter is the us we tend to cause most of our own problems by putting ourselves in positions we should not be in. So, then what does God do with us then? It's simple, He tests us to see how we are going to respond.

I know it sounds far-fetched but it's the truth. It's in the test of the trial that builds your greatest education. It's in education that builds character. Every storm is a trial. The test is to see if when things get hard are we going to trust in God and run to Him for the answer and not waiver or give up. We are to keep fighting the good fight of faith and hope in God in every situation, every problem. We need to know that he will work it all out for our good.

He wants to see while we are going through the trial that we learn from it also. None of us are cruising through this life without problems. Another test is given to see if we will rely on Him completely. So, that's when we would need to work on patience. By this I mean sometimes it may be tough to have patience when you feel as if your world is crashing down before you, but patience is a big test. That's where you will do battle in prayer for that time and time again. (Romans 5:3-4).

Another reason why you feel shipwrecked is that maybe you're following the crowd. It may be that the attitude is that everyone else does this so I should too. But that's not biblical and that may cause the problem to get much worse. Never follow the crowd because most of the time that crowd will lead you down a dark alley. That will leave you feeling like you're drowning. The best thing you can start to do now is this don't go drifting away by that it means don't give up ever. Don't throw away the people who are in your life, could be relationships or friendships or in other words don't quit or abandon you ship always stay with it. It's very easy to self-isolate but it's not healthy to do this so don't consider it. If you do this and continue to be persistent you will set sail and be much happier and you will be blessed. God wants to bless His children and wants the very best for us. He truly has our best interest at heart. He doesn't want us to sink in any way so once you learn these simple steps life will become much easier in coping with everyday living. He never said there wouldn't be any storms in our lives, but He does promise to be with us in the storms.

Walking that straight and narrow road requires a great deal of perseverance and battles that for me personal that I have learned throughout my years of being a Christian. Most of my battles I had took place in my prayer life. I had to pray consistently day and night and stay in tune with my Heavenly Father for my prayers to just reach heaven and to get answered. Reading the Word and living with the Word also. Most people today have different views of that, they may feel that they can read, pray and go and do whatever they choose and live the way they want without any regard to what's pleasing to the Lord, instead they do what's pleasing to the flesh. You must put away the "old" man and put on the "new" man, especially if you claim you to be in the will of God.

Putting on means the old must die and the new is born so when you accept Jesus as your Lord and Savior you become new as a new birth your spirit in you is reborn. Example John (3:3) So therefore the things you used to do you no longer want to do and those places that you used to go you don't want to go anymore. You soon will lose all desire for things of your past life and live for God now. This is how you start to set sail for your life. Your life as a new believer. Anchor your faith in Jesus let Him steer your ship.

"We walk by Faith and not by Sight." We have all heard this time and time again but what does this really mean? For this I tell you not to judge or mislead anyone, but to simply make this as easy as I can to explain what this term means. In the book of Hebrews (11:1-6) it gives the best scripture of it. Now faith is the substance of things hoped for, the evidence of things not seen. Without faith it is impossible to please God but then it goes on to say that we must believe that he is a rewarder of them that diligently seek him. So let me break this down. We all can look up and see a blue sky and feel the wind blowing in the sky, but we know not where it comes, but we believe anyway. That's faith in knowing that the wind is going to come no matter what. It is a certain knowing even if we don't physically see it. We know it comes from somewhere up in the sky above. We never saw Jesus, but we believe He is there. When we pray, we know that our Heavenly Father is listening to our heart's deepest cries. It's knowing that in the spirit realm all things are being worked out. On the other side, we have angels fighting for us making things happen by defending us daily. We can't see them, but they are there. In heaven the angels are protecting and doing the work that they are assigned by God to do although we cannot see this in the natural but in the spirit realm this is what is happening in the heavens. This is faith it's the believing in the unseen things in which we all must hold on to for our hope that makes up for all our belief systems and that states our ground for our role as being a follower of Christ. We don't go by what the natural eyes see because that is not the real reality of the situation at hand. By this I mean there is a plan that was well orchestrated by Jesus even before you were born, and that plan was already written in the book that is called *The Lamb's Book of Life*.

In this book God Himself designed for each person to one day be revealed. In this book for starters those of us who are saved from grace born again accepted Jesus in their hearts have their name in this book. There are events of everything in that person's life from birth until death recorded. The story of your past, present and all the good, bad and the forgiven are all part of his plan. The mistakes you made along the way on the journey you were on during your life are also recorded. But then in big red letters I truly believe that it says, "SINS WASHED AWAY REDEEMED BY THE BLOOD OF THE LAMB." Your name is next to it. There isn't going to be a turn of events that are going to be unnoticed by JESUS. He sees everything you do, and he is all knowing of it. You cannot hide anything from Him or escape Him from finding out your biggest secrets, because He is everywhere all the time. He has the whole heavens and earth in the palm of His hands, so he has it all under control. It may not look like it in the world we are living in today, but His mighty hand is holding it all.

Will you today give him your all? He is there waiting for you to make the decision to seek him diligently. His plan for you is good, it's not going to harm you it will give you hope and a future that you can truly appreciate knowing Him. Whatever is troubling your heart today? Take it to the Lord in prayer. My dear friend, I cannot express how important prayer is in your walk but if you dedicate time for God each day, He will show Himself faithful to you. Just as He did for me. It helps you grow spiritually mature in your faith as well as feeding your spirit, soul and mind. Prayer changes everything. It is the direct line to Jesus. Will you call on Him? Even the simplest prayer like "help me" is all it takes; they are called short prayers. Short prayers in some cases are just as important and strong as long-drawn-out ones. Even if they are sufficient.

The most important thing to remember is that you make a contact with God sometime during the day and night to keep the line of communication open. You ask "why?" Because it matters to God that he hears from you. He calls you "friend." So, to be a friend back you want to keep in contact. Also, there may be something he may want to say to you also. Pray and listen to your spirit too. We all look back at our lives and reflect on some point. For me personally, when I look as far back as I can remember I always remembered the goodness of God. Here is my story it's for the glory of God that I tell my story the way it was intended to be told. So, let the truth be told. Over the next chapter I'm going to let out some very detailed circumstances that took place during my journey.

It started when I was a very young girl, which was about the age of eight when I came to know the Lord. This all took place because when my mom and dad were divorced, I was only three years old. My mom had 2 children, myself and my brother who is seven years older than me. My dad after twelve years of marriage decided he no longer wanted to be married to my mom, so he just left her with two children. My mom tried very hard to fight the courts to get child support but was unsuccessful at the least. She received nothing. She had no choice but to apply for welfare so that we could eat. We were very poor growing up and that was difficult most of the time.

The emotional drama that took place from both of my parents fighting over money was devastating for any child to hear let alone be associated with. They both had their arguments, and the kids were always in the middle of that outcome. As a result, we were the ones who were hurt the most. My dad stopped coming around totally when I was twelve. I can remember asking him to give me a few dollars so that I could go have lunch with my friends at McDonald's on that Saturday afternoon. My Dad's response was, "Why don't you go and get a job at that McDonald's while you're at it because I am not giving you or your mother any money." With that was exactly what I had to do. Soon after that I went to my school and spoke to my guidance counselor to get working papers and that's how it all started for me. I've worked my whole life until I was forty-seven years old.

When I was growing up into my teens we were living in my grandmother's house because my mom took care of my grandmother because she had had a stroke and was paralyzed and in a wheelchair. She needed twenty-four hours around the clock care taking, so my mom and I were there as much as she needed. Several years later my grandmother passed away. Now just to give you the rundown of my mom's family history, my grandparents were wealthy people. My grandfather, in which I never met had a construction business and he taught the grandkids the business. So, they were a wealthy family.

My mom had seven brothers and sisters in total. Which made my grandmother have fourteen grandchildren. We all come from and Italian background. My aunts and uncles all had their own property.

When things were all finalized with the death of my grandmother the two of the children who oversaw the estate couldn't run fast enough to the bank to withdraw all the money from the accounts along with cashing several checks that she had hidden under the mattress. While she was barely coherent, they literally put the pen in her hand and changed her original will. In the new will it would read something like my mom would be left no property and money either. They cut my mom completely out of the will. Without anyone knowing. What they also did to my mom was horrific and shouldn't happen to anyone ever. They took a second mortgage out on a home that my grandfather had given to my mom when she first got married to my father. They made my mom pay them back over seventy thousand dollars for a home that was already paid for. This was the home I lived in before we moved into my grandmother's house. Unfortunately, my mom tried contacting attorneys and found there was nothing she could have done. Prior to this they asked my mom for a signature for something, and she didn't quite understand what she was reading because she was going through a lot. My mom remarried when I was thirteen years old and the man, she married had been diagnosed with cancer two years after they were married. She obviously had a lot to deal with on her plate and was lied to by her own family to sign this document. A few years later, when all was said and done grandmother passed, stepfather passes also my mom needed a place to live she asked for an apartment building to live from her brothers and sisters thinking they would maybe help her, but they told her, "No, you need to leave the block!" My mom was truly devastated as this for many years. All the money they had they would not help their own sister. They always made fun of her and called her "The Cinderella" of the family. It was a joke to them, but it hurt my mom more than you can ever know.

We then moved off the block and moved on with our lives. Forgetting that we all once had the perfect Italian family with good times on holidays and great summertime fun at my pool. The house we lived in was the largest house on the block and it had thirteen rooms. But nevertheless, the truth was I was the poorest person on the block living in the richest house on the top of the hill. Growing up being raised on welfare with no dad of my own to help me grow up was extremely tough for me. Talk about everything is not as it seems. The kids on the block and the next street were always making fun of me and persecuting me because I decided to go to a Christian church. I was in church three times a week and that included Sunday, morning and evening. I loved it there and that was where I first found the Lord. When I walked into the church for the first time, I felt so much love I couldn't believe it myself. Everyone was so nice and loving towards me. I never felt that before. They took me in and prayed with me, which lead me into saying the sinner's prayer to accept Jesus as the Savior in my heart. It was right there that I was saved! "Hallelujah, praise the Lord, thank you, Jesus."

In my adult years, I have always wanted to be part of a church and get involved and very well rooted in a place that I can call my home "church," so I stayed long enough in one church until I felt it was my time to move and that time for me was in 2017. I was introduced to the church I attend now. Since then, I have moved up the ladder within the congregation and now I'm serving as a Commissioned Minister. I received my certificate in July 2023. God has been working through me and for me in so many ways he has blessed me greatly. In September 2022, I went on another cruise to the Bahamas.

While I was in the water of the Caribbean, I was looking for coral and I found silver bars under the weeds of the ocean floor. I was using a metal detector to find any metals and was fortunate to find such treasures. I was so happy just to find something that was from a shipwreck many years ago. Another thing the Lord did for me was we had great weather too. You can never take for granted the condition of the ocean because sometimes you can get a rocky boat and that can make you seasick if you're not used to being out on the water. So, I always prayed for good weather before I get onboard.

I also was able to pay off my 2020 Kia Forte. I never thought I would ever have my own car "paid in full." Debt free at last. I owe it all to Yeshua/Jesus. He truly has provided for me every step of the way.

I'm already booked to go on my third cruise this September again. I'm going to try to find some gold this time with my very own metal detector. I leave in two weeks, and I cannot wait. I'm very excited and I have a lot to celebrate so far. I know that Jesus is still writing my story and he isn't finished with it yet. I look forward to seeing what new doors open for me and I'm still praying for my own apartment to come, and I know that when God is ready, he will open that door. I'm learning to just be still now and wait for all things to just come to pass. In my waiting I am very obedient to the Lord. I'm reading all books in my Bible now, too.

Along life's journey we all have one thing in common and that is that we all will get to our destiny. Meaning the end game of life. You may ask yourself *what do you mean by that?* What is destiny? Well, my friend, I'm here to tell you that we all want to get to heaven at the end of the road. We take all different roads in life but at the end of this life you will no doubt meet your maker. So, my question to you is this? Do you know Jesus? Does He know you? Without knowing Him you cannot and will not see the kingdom of God which is called Heaven. The Bible is very clear of this in John (3:4-5).

He stands at the door of your heart and knocks, and He is just waiting for you to let Him in. He will forgive you of all your sins and there isn't a sin He doesn't know about. He is going to remove all your iniquity as far is the east is and as far as the west is to be forgotten forevermore. Invite Him into your heart, it will be the best decision you will ever make in your entire life.

When I had a moment to really analyze the past few years of my life, I was certain of a few things that I wrote earlier of the enemy working overtime to distract me. It wasn't as if I was used to this because it was all new to me in the way that He was trying to invade my space. You see there is a place deep in your heart that only God dwells which is the soul that should remain free from the outside interferences. Otherwise, outside distractions. People who can become within your environment can either make or take away your joy. By this I mean that everyone on planet earth has some sort of problem, however... We must all remember to take it to the Lord in prayer, before exploding it out onto everyone like an erupting volcano. We must give an honest evaluation of every situation before giving advice to someone who is in need. Because in some cases if it's not what they want to hear they may feel that you're judging them and that will turn a good conversation into a bad one in zero to a second. Then, after that you have taken away what I call a joyful moment. So, with the enemy had been working hard at using people to influence me with talk and manipulation to bring me down. He also tried to make me think that I wasn't going to move forward and progress in which he was completely wrong. He tries to get inside your head, but the main thing is we cannot allow him to get into our" heads at all. Not even a little bit. If he sees he has a way in he will take over and have control over your mind, then he's got you! So, we must stand against all principalities of darkness that revolt against us. Tearing down strongholds.

To be healed and delivered from whatever it is your facing today, first seek God and His Kingdom then all things will be added to you. Second, is you must be willing to let the Lord really work inside of you from the inside out. And what I mean by this, is that you need to completely surrender it all to Him! Everything not just a little of it, or half of it, all of it. You must know what it's like to be broken before your Heavenly Father so that He can get to those places deep inside that no one sees someone even knows. Then the healing process will begin. Notice I say process because it isn't the best author there is, and He is writing your story with you on His mind because He loves us.

I have done this many times in prayer. It's been proven to work every time. Here is the main key... Build an altar, build a prayer life, stay in constant conversation with Jesus throughout the day and night. I will never stop talking about the goodness of God and how good He has been to me in my entire life. Since February of 2022 I have been so blessed to have been able to go on three cruises so far. Some of this book was written while and during that time in which I was truly inspired to write this book. It has been a privilege for me to share my very own experiences and a well-deserved journey. So, my last words of encouragement are this... Let Jesus work through you, and in you. Stay in His will for your life. You won't regret it. I'm so happy that you read my book. I hope it helped you in many ways. I would like to leave you with one final thought, some may say that God is there in the eye of the storm however I would like to change that to God is there in the beginning, middle and the end of all storms. He's always in control, He is my anchor!

The End.

About the Author

This story is about the journey of how a young girl grew up in a small town and how she became a Christian. Growing up in a single parent household was incredibly challenging for her. She endured many trials, and tribulations which taught her in life how to persevere, overcome and triumph over some of the hardest things, with Jesus as her anchor. Weathering each storm, she realizes that even when the sails are torn, and the winds blow and you're out on the sea and you think you're all alone, God was by her side all the time. Trusting in the only love she knew as her heavenly Father teaches her His provision, and His calling for her life as she learns how to completely give in to His will.

Milton Keynes UK
Ingram Content Group UK Ltd.
UKHW050717010724
444982UK00014B/924